First published in the UK in 2018

Cover image created by Igor Yanchenko.

Find the Fibro Guy online at www.thefibroguy.com

ISBN 978-1-9996044-2-4

eISBN 978-1-9996044-1-7

Contents

Acknowledgements 7

Part One 8

Introduction 9

  How this Book is Structured 11

Adam's Story 21

Mairi's story 24

Fibro Chicken 29

Introducing My Inputs and Outputs 35

  How We Used to Think About Pain 39

  Pain is an Output 41

Inputs and Outputs in Action 43

  What is Pain For? 47

  How Chronic Pain is Processed 49

  Protection Output 50

  Belief Reinforcing Output 52

  Mood Output 55

  Subsidiary Output 57

  Belief Dismantling Output 59

  Getting Stuck in Protection Output Mode 63

Using Inputs and Outputs to Understand Pain 65

The Impact of Previous Knowledge ... 65
Making Sense of What We Encounter ... 67
How You Cope Affects How You Cope ... 72
What About the Other Symptoms of Fibro? ... 77
The Spoon Theory ... 77
Fibro Fog ... 79
Sleep ... 80
Bowels ... 81
Itching ... 82
Being Plastic ... 84
Bioplasticity in Action ... 84
Research Evidence for Bioplasticity ... 87
Part Two ... 92
Getting Ready to Get Better ... 93
What We Know So Far ... 93
Your Story of Recovery ... 98
Support groups ... 101
Barriers to Recovery ... 101
Evidence For and Against ... 103
Why is this Treatment Not Available on the NHS? ... 109
A Word About Procrastination ... 115
Getting Things Done ... 116

Making a Start 118
Worrying About Moving 120
Client Success Stories and Testimonials 123
Steph - Myalgic Encephalomyelitis 123
Carly - Hypermobile Ehlers-Danlos Syndrome 125
Richard - Fibromyalgia 128
Stronger Than You Think 131
Muscles are not the Only Strong Ones 131
Strength Experiment 132
Age Related Concerns 133
The Myth of the “Weak Core” 135
Impact of Belief on Levels of Pain 138
Part Three 142
Magic Movement 143
Unhelpful Associations 148
Pie 153
Pre-Foundation 159
Building your foundation 162
Wellness is Your Absolute Priority 162
Wake Up, Shake Up and Stay Up 165
Cold Showers 166
Everyday Movement 172

Sensory Turn Downs 173
Kneeling Hip Flexor Complex Stretch 175
How to do it 177
Movements 178
Lean Overs 179
Hinge Pattern 180
How to hinge 182
Legs Up the Wall 183
Descending Modulation (Pin and Press) 185
How to Pin and Press 187
Progress Check 190
Learning to Walk Again 191
Museum Walking 191
But What if I Flare Up? 196
D-Day 200
Upon Waking Up 200
Shower 201
Evaluate and Jot Down 202
Breakfast 203
Sensory Turn Downs, Daily Movements and P+P 205
Time to F.E.A.S.T. 207
Reflect and Jot Down 207

It's Your Move....209

Bibliography....213

Acknowledgements

Adam:

I thank my beautiful partner Seren for her unrelenting support in my mission to create a future free of chronic pain. I would also like to thank the many wonderful clients I have had the pleasure to work with over the years and to those that helped to keep my passion for the job burning bright all these years.

Mairi:

This book is dedicated to my amazing father Keith who endured great pain, always with dignity, good humour and love.

Part One

Introduction

Mairi: They told me that fibromyalgia was an untreatable disease, that nobody knew what caused it, no one knew why it happened to people and that a cure would therefore be impossible. They told me that fibro symptoms would often come on after a traumatic life event, either physical or emotional, and in my case, it came swiftly after the loss of my son. For me, there was a link between the emotional trauma of bereavement and the physical agony of fibromyalgia. There was, however, no clinical cause for my pain. I didn't have any physical injury, no tissue damage or any pathological reason why I might be experiencing all my suffering. I had tried many things over the years to help with the pain, but having been through failed treatment after failed treatment, I felt like giving up. With no identifiable cause and no recognised cure, I eventually found myself on the 7:45am Edinburgh-Newcastle train to see someone who apparently knew what was going on with this horrible experience. At 8:00am, the pain caused by unloading my laptop from my back pack on the train was so severe it reduced me to tears. Just a few hours later, at 11:45am, I had flipped a 105kg tyre and felt absolutely fine about it. Over the next few weeks of working with Adam, I reversed my symptoms and began to live my life again.

As a psychologist, I was amazed at what a slightly scary ex-soldier with nothing more than a GCSE in art behind him had managed to create. I needed to find out more about what had actually happened to me and to the hundreds of other people who have recovered from chronic pain. I needed to know if this recovery would last. Most importantly I needed to know how and why this approach had worked. Adam and I are good friends now and we wrote this book together to help people understand that with the right knowledge and a desire to change, recovery is possible.

The book is set out in three sections. The first part explains what fibromyalgia really is – a label for a set of symptoms that cannot be explained by any other diagnosis. It describes why chronic pain with no apparent physical cause is different to the pain that a person would normally feel after illness or injury. It's crucial that people who are living with chronic pain know why they feel this way before they start out trying to change their lives. Some of the information will be difficult to take on board as it will go against what you might have thought all your life. Depending on their background and specialty, it may even challenge what your medical support team believe. The information we present in this book is based on the latest cutting-edge research which is being carried out right now, in medical and academic centres worldwide. It is not plucked out of thin air but is based on real clinical evidence produced by experts in a variety of medical fields.

At times it's hard to accept this new way of thinking about pain so please do take the time to really get to grips with the first part of the book. If you have any questions we are happy to help. Please contact us directly using the contact details on Adam's website www.thefibroguy.com. We promise to read every question we are sent and will do our best to either answer the question directly or signpost you to someone who can help.

Please be absolutely clear on one thing: we are not suggesting at any time that the pain and other symptoms you are experiencing are imagined or made up. Your pain is very real and we know this because we have both been there. What we do not accept is the convenient fibromyalgia "label" that is applied to people who are experiencing the pain. This acceptance of this label allows you to be parked on a shelf with a "diagnosis" that means you have no access to effective treatment and you are likely to suffer your current level of pain, or worse, for the rest of your life. We challenge this way of thinking by helping people to understand what chronic pain is and why it is caused. Once you know this, you can take steps towards getting better and getting your life back. We know your pain is real, but it can be reduced or eliminated altogether with the correct approach. Some people believe that the fibromyalgia label is helpful because it lets them access sources of support that they cannot access without a diagnosis. This support is crucial for people who are suffering with severe chronic pain to help them survive on a day to day basis. Along with the label, however, comes a need to accept that there is no cure and no treatment for the chronic pain that is being endured. This is simply not true. Once again let's be clear. We are not saying that the pain is not real. We are saying that labelling the symptoms and putting people's lives in the trashcan of fibromyalgia is unacceptable and needs to end.

How this Book is Structured

The first section of the book begins with a bit of background to Adam and my experiences that brought us into the world of chronic pain. We have both suffered tremendous levels of pain, day in day out. We have lost years of our lives to pain, and we have missed out on significant events and opportunities because of it. Our relationships with loved ones have fundamentally changed because we were living with chronic pain. All of this happened alongside the judgement by others that a person with chronic pain lives with every day. Like you, we have been disbelieved. We have been told there is nothing wrong with us, that we need to pull ourselves together and get on with life and that everybody feels pain sometimes, we just need to man up. We have shared our own stories to show that we know what it's like to live with chronic pain. We've both been there, believe me. We understand the life of a chronic pain sufferer and we both know how hard it is to get your life back after a diagnosis of fibromyalgia. We hope that our stories help you to understand why we were determined to get better and that these stories encourage you to do the same.

The chapter titled "Fibro Chicken" is a light- hearted story which shows that how you understand and make sense of life is influenced by what you already know and what you have experienced previously. We hope you remember it when you're reading the following chapters which may well challenge your fundamental beliefs about pain and its role in our human experience

The chapter "Introducing My Inputs and Outputs" explains one of the core components of Adam's method of recovering from fibromyalgia. It explains how our brains make sense of everyday experiences and how our knowledge and what happens to us during our lives influences our daily experiences.

“Inputs and Outputs in Action” is the chapter which takes each type of output in turn, describing their function, how and why they occur and how they contribute to the experience of chronic pain.

The chapter “Using Inputs and Outputs to Understand Pain” takes this information to the next step. Once we understand how we make sense of the world generally, we can focus in on how we make sense of our physical sensations and this helps us to understand why we feel pain. Once we understand what is happening, we can begin to think about how we can change this and reduce or eliminate the suffering of chronic pain.

We then consider “What About the Other Symptoms of Fibro?”. The label of fibromyalgia covers not just the chronic pain, but other symptoms such as ongoing fatigue. This chapter suggests why the collection of symptoms might occur and how they are linked to the pain which is at the core of the experience.

“Being Plastic” describes how the human body and brain can adapt and helps us to understand how we can take control of our lives in order to help ourselves get better. We are designed to be well as our default state and this chapter explains how we can use what happens naturally to help us recover from the everyday pain we feel.

The second section of the book explains why and how recovery from chronic pain is possible. Reading this book will be challenging, not just in terms of understanding what is happening to you. Some of your core beliefs will be turned upside down and what you have known about the world until now will change. This is difficult and scary and the chapter "Getting Ready to Get Better" aims to help you prepare for the challenges ahead. The chapter explains what to expect, good and bad, as you begin your recovery from chronic pain.

The chapter on "Support Groups" is a difficult one, both to write and to read. The support group I joined online helped me in my darkest hours and without it, I'm not even sure I would be here now. The people I met through the group have been so kind and helpful and I admire their endurance and tenacity and hope they are able to find their own routes to wellness. Sometimes, however, a group of people who are suffering from the same ailments can find it challenging when one of their own breaks free. We hope this chapter deals with this situation sympathetically. It has been included in the book to help those who take on the challenges they face in recovering to understand why this recovery might be difficult for others to accept.

One question that we are often asked is "Why is This Treatment Not Available on the NHS?" and the chapter with this title aims to answer that question. We hope, in time, that the approach we recommend for recovery from chronic pain becomes the norm. This chapter explains why that might take a while.

We both know how hard it is to take on the challenge of getting better and "A Word About Procrastination" is there to hopefully help you address some of the barriers that might be stopping you from getting on with it. It will be difficult, and you may well try to talk yourself out of what you need to do to recover. If you get around to reading this chapter, you will hopefully make it to the final section of the book which calls you to action.

The "Client Success Stories and Testimonials" chapter tells how some of the hundreds of people have recovered from chronic pain with Adam's help. These stories are written in the own words of the people who recovered. The names that are given are the real names of those who were happy to share their experiences. These are just a small fraction of the success stories we hear every day and we hope they inspire you to be part of this recovery movement.

The chapter "Stronger Than You Think" was written to help you gather your thoughts on recovery, pulling together everything you've learned so far to make recovery possible. We hope it will encourage you to start your own recovery and to take on the challenges of the final section of the book.

The third section deals with the nuts and bolts of what you need to do to recover from chronic pain. "Magic Movement" is the first step and this chapter spills the beans on what you need to know to get your life back after the fibromyalgia diagnosis. It is the first step that Adam wants everyone to take; to know the truth about "so called" magic movements.

Getting better is going to need a lot of hard work on your part and some of that is not going to be easy. "Unhelpful Associations" will let you see what is holding you back and where your previous thoughts and experiences have shaped your current situation. The contents of this chapter will help you to work out how to deal with some of the barriers you encounter on your journey to wellness.

Adam wrote the chapter titled "Pie" to explain how the different slices of life interact. That's all I can say. Enjoy!

The "Pre-foundation" chapter will get you ready to make the movements which will potentially be life changing for you. It will set the scene for the work to come and explain what to expect as you begin the programme.

When you are ready to make that start, "Building Your Foundation" will take you through the two-week foundation programme in detail. In this chapter, you will learn the details of the steps involved in the programme, including a description of how to do the recommended movements.

If I could choose the one thing that meant more to me than anything else within the programme it was "Learning to Walk Again". Who knew that there are different ways to walk and that your pain may be causing your immobility? Now it makes perfect sense, of course, but when I was struggling with pain and fatigue, I couldn't seem to find a way to get mobile without making my situation worse. This chapter will tell you all you need to know to get walking again.

One question that Adam gets asked regularly is "But What if I Flare Up?". In this chapter, Adam explains why this may have happened in the past and why it is unlikely to be an issue if you follow the programme carefully. Given what you will have read by the time you get to this chapter, you'll be able to control your movements to avoid any possibility of overexertion.

Day one of starting on the programme is detailed in the chapter titled "D-Day". This is the chapter that gives you the itinerary to follow on the first day of your journey towards wellness. Follow it carefully and the rest of the programme will just fall into place!

So much will change in your life when you make the movements towards wellness, and the chapter to help you maintain your new lifestyle is titled "Time to F.E.A.S.T." Wellness is your number one priority from now on, and to sustain it, follow Adam's advice for enriching your everyday experiences. This will help you to maintain your new lifestyle and lead a happy and active life. Ultimately, this will help you to find ways to change from a person who suffers with chronic pain to a person who lives pain-free, forever.

"It's Your Move" is the chapter that reminds you that you will only recover by the choices you make. We hope that what you read will help you take on the challenge of recovery and join the hundreds of people who no longer carry the fibromyalgia label, but lead full active lives once again.

Disclaimer

The training, information and instructional components of this book are to be taken as information and not medical advice. Always consult a medical professional before partaking in any physical activity. "The Fibro Guy™", "Adam Foster" and "Dr Mairi Harper" take no responsibility for any loss or injury sustained during the participation of the physical components of this book.

Adam's Story

I know first-hand of the difficulties that those in chronic pain face, being a sufferer myself many years ago. In 2009, I was involved in an I.E.D. blast whilst serving in Afghanistan with the Household Cavalry regiment. Members of my troop received both minor and major injuries, but I escaped relatively unharmed with only slight whiplash. A few months later, I returned to civilian life after my 2009 tour of duty had ended. However, a few months into civilian life, I became increasingly unwell, developing constant migraines, tension headaches, fatigue and pain. Pain which soon became classed as chronic.

After frustratingly being passed from specialist to specialist, I was told about many different "root causes" for my pain. I was told by my GP it was more than likely due to Post Traumatic Stress Disorder. A physiotherapist told me it was my bad posture. This was even though I'd done numerous ceremonial duties on horseback, such as trooping the colour, which requires almost perfect posture. I found that experience significantly more painful than slouching! An osteopath told me that all my problems where down to a sluggish lymphatic system and it was because I wasn't moving enough, despite the fact at this point, I was still running a few miles a day. Every man and his dog were keen to give me a simple cause for the pain and eventually, a chiropractor deemed that the most likely cause of my pain was scar tissue formation from my previous injuries. This was the explanation I was given for why I would suffer from daily headaches and more migraines than you could shake a stick at, as well as explaining the fatigue and chronic pain. I lived with the constant fear that the slightest movement would injure my neck further and possibly leave me paralyzed. At that point in my life, this explanation for my pain seemed the most plausible and this is the one that I reluctantly accepted. The posture explanation seemed redundant, the PTSD explanation is something I didn't want to accept due to the stigma, but scar tissue, that was something that validated my pain and one explanation I could get behind. However, accepting this diagnosis was probably the worst thing I could have done at that point, as almost immediately, the pain got worse. The more I read about it, the more symptoms I exhibited and eventually I hit rock bottom.

At my very lowest point, when I had exhausted every possible resource, alternative therapy, tried every pill, potion, every gel, treatment, and counselling option, I almost gave up. After finally realising that although the large amounts of Tramadol I was using and the expensive and frequent chiropractic sessions did allow me to struggle on and still actually work, they were ultimately only masking the pain and causing more cognitive problems than I had initially thought they would. I quickly realised I had to do something about it. I understood that the NHS was far too stretched and too tightly governed to be able to help me. I had seen the specialists who were available to me and they had provided me with nothing. So, I was left with one choice and, being from a military background, I did what I had been trained to do. I chose to improvise, adapt and overcome. The first port of call, I thought, should be to understand the body, my mind and more about what pain actually is. I set out to educate myself on human anatomy, pain, biomechanics, psychology, connective tissue and human movement as whole. Over the next year, I created a programme that addressed the root causes of my problems, or at least what I perceived them to be at the time. In doing so, I got my life back and over the next few years, I used my programme to help many other people. A little later down the line, I was presented with new information that completely destroyed how I thought my programme actually worked. This wasn't the greatest feeling in the world and much to my dismay, I realised, that "how" I had recovered and indeed how I had helped others to recovery, could not possibly be true. The mechanisms of how I thought it had helped had been destroyed. This was the singularity to my big bang. Every success you see in the press, on the page and indeed even Mairi, is the result of this turning point in my life. After realising that I had been so wrong, another world opened up for me and by letting go of everything I thought I knew, I was able to learn far more. In turn, I was able to help more people than I ever imagined. As you read through this book, I hope you can do the same.

Mairi's story

I first realised something was physically wrong in summer 2008. I noticed that, when I woke up in the morning, my legs were stiff and aching. We had just welcomed a new puppy into the family so I presumed this was the result of me walking more than usual and didn't think much more about it. A few months later when the pain in the morning was worse, I realised that this couldn't be put down to the dog walks but like most busy mums would do, I decided to ignore it and hope it went away. I was studying for my PhD in psychology at the time and I spent a lot of the day hunched up over a computer, reading and writing for long periods of time. I began noticing that my arms were getting sore from the back of my hands to my elbows and that my migraines were getting more common. A trip to the optician found nothing wrong with my eyesight so I put the pain down to bad posture and overwork. I was totally committed to my studies so there was no way I would consider changing what I was doing so once again, I decided to put up and shut up.

As 2009 progressed, however, the pain levels crept up and up. Walking was very painful and seemed to be getting steadily worse. My arms were so sore that I couldn't lift the big academic books without searing pain and trying to work through the migraine pain was excruciating. By now I was a single mum of three and working several part time jobs to earn enough to support the family during my studies. I couldn't afford to be ill and my young family needed a mum who could function normally. Reluctantly, I consulted my GP who carried out all the tests he could think of to rule out any diagnosable condition. After a few months, I was formally diagnosed with fibromyalgia, along with the PTSD, anxiety and depression I'd had since the tragic loss of my young son in 1999.

I was prescribed pain relief in the form of strong opioids and warned that these were highly addictive, but that I'd be ok so long as I limited them to a maximum of eight tablets per day. These helped reduce the pain although it was never completely taken away, but they came with their own set of side effects. My tummy had never been great but now I could add Irritable Bowel Syndrome to my selection box of diagnoses. Bunged up or super loose, my bowels were not my best friend it's fair to say! If I needed to go to the loo, I had to go immediately, so being out of the house was always a bit of a worry. Long journeys were fraught with dangers! Not to mention the pain that went along with sitting in the same position for hours on end. Driving made the pain in my arms and my legs worse, but public transport meant the possibility of standing or waiting in the cold, both of which would trigger a flare up of pain that would last days or even weeks. I had to leave a job I loved to move back to my home town, hoping that the support of friends and family would ease the burden a bit. Still a single parent and therefore the breadwinner for the family, I needed to work full time to support us but the job I secured was highly stressful and my employers didn't seem to believe that there was anything wrong with me. I was frequently told that if I struggled to do my job there were plenty of other people who would be happy to take it from me, so I pushed on through the pain and fatigue, relying heavily on medication to prop me up. This led to an inevitable crash and burn where the pain was so excruciating the only relief to be had was with morphine. Once the worst was over I would head back to work in fear of losing my job, only to face the next build-up of pain, fatigue and stress which would then lead to the inevitable flare up. After months of intermittent absences and an overall deterioration in symptoms, I decided to leave the job and return to a part time position I had held whist working on my PhD.

The improvement was almost immediate. My confidence was pretty low, but I enjoyed the job and seemed to be making a positive difference, so gradually my mood improved. The pain and fatigue lessened considerably, clearly showing me the link between the symptoms and overall stress levels. Then, out of the blue, a once in a lifetime job opportunity came up and I wondered, just maybe, could this be my happy ending? Not daring to hope that I might be in with a chance, I applied, and to my utter astonishment, I was offered the job! It felt like all my Christmases had come at once – the best job, the best colleagues and the best employer I could possibly imagine. Well paid, challenging and fun. It doesn't get any better than this. On a high, I moved into my lovely office and got to know the team I was joining. They couldn't have been more supportive, and I knew I would learn so much from them, both professionally and personally. But this horrible condition hadn't gone away, it was just lurking beneath the surface, ready to destroy everything I'd hoped and dreamed of. Within a few months, the familiar pain was coursing through me, the painkillers were only taking the top off the pain and my brain was becoming increasingly fuzzy. Following the advice to pace myself, I did as much work as I could before going home exhausted each day. My children were having to do so much more for themselves and were getting used to a mum who was becoming increasingly disabled. Inevitably, the pain worsened again, and I was absent from work for months at a time. I tried so hard to find a way to get better, reading every article and book I could find. I tried dozens of dietary supplements, various electrical zapping machines, massage, heat treatments, scented oils, meditation, you name it, all to no avail. Whilst I might be able to get a day or two of relief, nothing provided any type of ongoing remission. I married a man who has proven to be a very supportive husband, never complaining about pushing me in the wheelchair that I now needed to be mobile. Devastated, I finally accepted that my academic career was over and what little activity level I had would be dedicated to supporting my family in whatever way I could. I resigned from the job of my dreams with the expectation of a lifetime of pain, exhaustion and confusion. If I'd been an animal, it would have been a kindness to put me out of my misery. And then, by pure chance, I found the Facebook page of The Fibro Guy. And I wondered...

By the time I first met Adam, I'd had eight years of severe pain in my arms and legs, and migraines for as long as I can remember. This was definitely chronic pain: every day, disabling and demoralizing, with flare ups of extreme agony occurring throughout the year. Along with this pain came the numbing fatigue. My sleep patterns were never great but as the symptoms worsened, I would wake several times in the night. Of course, this would make me sleepy the next day but the fatigue that I experienced was more than that. It was like wearing a lead suit, always feeling a deep sense of exhaustion where all I wanted was to just close my eyes and sleep. No matter whether I did get some sleep or not, the exhaustion levels stayed the same. But for me one of the worst things was the "fibro fog". The confusion, forgetting things, not able to concentrate to get anything done. My mental fitness was tested, and I scored levels that would be found in someone with early dementia. At 50 years old and after years of building an academic career this was totally soul destroying! I've never been a particularly sporty person but to not be able to read, make plans or even watch a movie without getting lost was really distressing.

Given the symptoms above I had thought recovery impossible, But I was wrong. Adam says, “To be right, you have to be wrong” and this really is the best place to start to explain how my recovery began.

Fibro Chicken

Adam: When I was five years old my Dad told me a joke: "Why did the chicken cross the road?". The answer to this, which we all know, is to get to the other side. Like most of you reading this, I was thoroughly un-entertained. "How is that funny?" I asked myself. What a terrible joke, I thought, and promptly forgot all about it.

Many years later whilst talking with a friend, I was told the same joke, "Why did the chicken cross the road?" the answer still being, as we all know, to get to the other side. Again, I was not impressed and my friend seeing my disappointed face slowly leant in closer and said," Oh you're one of the people who still doesn't get it". You see when you are five years old, or indeed any other age, you have a subjective view of the world. This is based on your own understanding of what you believe to be right and wrong, how things work, what means what or at least how you perceive it to be. So, when my friend smiled and said, "He wanted to get to the other side, as in the afterlife. It's a suicide joke about a chicken" it blew my mind! I had thought for all those years, that it was nothing more just a really bad joke with very little meaning. It was considered a joke because it was so literal and it was just simply terrible.

You see the five-year-old me viewed the world based on what he knew and at five years old I did not have a very good understanding of death or indeed the concept of an afterlife. I had lived for years being 100% sure I knew what this joke meant, and I would have argued until I was blue in the face that this joke was purely a literal joke.

However, with experience, new information and different beliefs, I could see the world differently. When I was now presented with new information, I could actually see the real meaning. There will be some people reading this who already knew this, but there will be so many more who had not even considered the meaning of the joke. At the moment, there are many things which you believe to be true, which are simply not true and this is the case for all of us. What Mairi and I want to do with this book is to give you the information that is missing, so that you can fully understand why the chicken crossed the road, or indeed, that recovery is an option....

If you are reading this then it's very likely you know all 26 letters of the alphabet. However, can you imagine if you only knew seven of the 26 letters. Do you think you would be able to read and write as well as you can now? Absolutely not! I had a similar experience with maths many years ago. I would avoid any form of simple arithmetic like the plague. I found maths incredibly hard and I demonised it until it started to negatively affect my life. Finally, after saying enough is enough and attending a few night classes, I soon realised that I found it quite easy. Knowledge about pain is no different. If you're missing important pieces of the puzzle, it becomes an untameable monster. So, going forward, we need to give you the missing information and avoid letting our old beliefs get in the way of our recovery.

Mairi: My contribution to this book is to reflect on my personal experience of recovery and to add the scientific evidence to support Adam's methods. As much as I love chickens, I'm going to avoid adding anything to the story above. For now, I think it would be useful to summarise the current medical position in the UK regarding what we know about fibromyalgia and what the NHS has decided to offer in terms of treatments for chronic pain.

In the UK we have a body called the National Institute for Health and Care Excellence, or NICE for short. This body publishes the best information we have about recognised medical conditions, so I have used this information to provide a short summary on the current position of knowledge about fibromyalgia at the time of writing (Spring 2018).

We believe that fibromyalgia has been diagnosed in between 2% and 6% of the population, though the prevalence of chronic pain it is likely to be higher as many people don't get a formal clinical diagnosis, despite feeling ongoing pain. Between 35% and 50% of adults in the UK are estimated to be living with chronic pain at any one time. It usually takes more than two years for a patient to be given a diagnosis and in practice, up to four specialists are consulted before diagnosis is confirmed. Fibromyalgia is defined as a complex set of symptoms including ongoing pain and fatigue, sleep that doesn't lead to the person feeling refreshed, depression, anxiety and the "fibro fog" – problems with memory and concentration. Women are ten times more likely to be affected than men. Most people notice the symptoms between the ages of 20 and 50 years old, though it can be found in children, young people and older adults. Some people believe there is a family link with the condition though this has not been widely studied. Stress often makes the symptoms worse.

Fibromyalgia Syndrome is the name given to a set of symptoms which occur where no other clinical explanation for the symptoms can be found. It is a diagnosis that is made by exclusion. This means that your health professional will test for other conditions that may explain your symptoms. If nothing is found and the symptoms remain, your condition will be labelled as fibromyalgia and voila! You have a diagnosis and the clinician's job is done. In terms of prognosis and what to expect in the future, your clinician does not expect your condition to be cured, but hopes to minimise the impact of symptoms by following the treatment recommendations. They will also know, however, that you are likely to experience a decline in your level of functioning, both from a physical and social perspective. Having a diagnosis of fibromyalgia will also probably affect your ability to work and you may need to work less hours, change your job, or even give up work altogether.

The medical guidelines state that patients will benefit from a prompt diagnosis and being given information about fibromyalgia. The advice is that treatment should take a "stepped" approach, so if the patient is still looking for help after receiving information, they should be offered physical therapy. If this doesn't help, drug treatments are offered. One of the key recommendations for treating fibromyalgia is the use of graded exercise to help reduce pain, improve wellbeing and help patients to be able to keep carrying out the activities of daily life. Well I don't know about you but the prospect of getting involved in any form of exercise filled me with horror! It's fair to say I've never been a natural athlete. Even as a child I hated games. I was good at swimming but my parents didn't encourage it. They thought I'd end up with a body like a Bavarian shotput athlete when what they really wanted was a slim, petite ballerina. Tough luck eh? (No offence to Bavarian shotput athletes). I didn't mind walking. That's what you did when I was kid, but it was only ever a means to an end (literally) not walking for the sake of getting fit. Don't get me wrong – I'd love to be fit. It's just the sweaty, sore, exhausting stuff you have to do to get there that puts me off. To be avoided at all costs. I never got that thing that people talk about – the rush of endorphins that makes you feel good after exercise. The only good feeling I got was when I knew that it was finished! And I just didn't believe that it would make a positive difference. I mean, I had tried a few things in the past but never seemed to get any fitter. I just got sweatier and even more tired. Euch. After suffering with years of chronic pain, the idea of any kind of exercise sounded like the worst idea ever! How could doing exercise even be possible, never mind being helpful in any way? However, I now know that this is the best way to deal with chronic pain. I may have mentioned my aversion to exercise to Adam on occasion (slight understatement here) and he suggested that I think about "movement" rather than "exercise". This has helped, especially when the movement has an additional benefit beyond "just" helping my condition. As a life-long low person of low self-esteem and typical mum, I tend to put my own needs right at the bottom of the list of things to do. If I have any time left after doing all the things that are necessary for the family, I might allow myself the odd few minutes to do something that I like or that makes me feel good about myself. If I can think about moving more to get things done like walking the dog, housework, pottering in the garden, I can justify the effort more easily than spending an evening at an exercise class. Before I met Adam and followed his programme, any of these things would have been impossible. I could barely walk a few feet without pain and exhaustion, but now I can do any of these exciting activities that I choose! As difficult as it may be to believe right now, moving more and in the right ways is definitely going to be helpful in keeping me well and hopefully, making me a bit fitter to get more out of life. I'm sure the prospect of this right now is going down as well as Adam's joke about the chicken. Once you have read the advice in this book, however, I hope your view changes, just as mind did. It's all about knowing, really knowing, why that darn chicken decided to cross the road to the other side.

Introducing My Inputs and Outputs

Adam: Have you ever wondered why no single treatment for a health condition works for everyone? Have you ever wondered why doing the things that used to fill you with joy, now cause you pain? Have you ever wondered why we experience EVERYTHING differently to other people? Well, Inputs and Outputs is why!

Whilst working with clients, I found it hard to explain how I had used the advancements in pain neuroscience research to fill in the blanks of my own recovery and how they could use this knowledge to recover, too. Pain consumes people. It makes focusing on anything else extremely difficult. So, I created an explanation using the Input Output methodology, to help explain why people experience chronic pain and why it doesn't go away despite many different treatments and responses to professional interventions. Over the years, with a lot of research, challenging work and loads of trial and error, I created my method that I use to help people. Whilst employing the Input Output methodology and using specific movements as a catalyst for change, I managed to teach people how to successfully recover from chronic pain. I had never thought It would help as many people as it has and when a psychologist recovers using it and wants to help spread its word, then it's time for something big. So, the first step of our journey, is to understand Inputs and Outputs.

The first thing I want you to do right now is to wiggle your toes or move a different part of your body. That's easy, right? That's the Conscious You, creating a conscious action. Now, I want you to try and release some adrenaline, just like you would do when a car speeds through a crossing you are about to walk over. Doesn't work does it? The Conscious You does not have the ability to control a subconscious act. Only the Subconscious You can do that. If someone later today jumps around a corner and scares you, the Subconscious You will flood your body with adrenaline fairly easily. But you can't make your body release it at will. In fact, most of the actions you do are subconscious. We have known since the 1970's that our subconscious minds start preparing a little over a third of a second before we actually consciously decide to act.

Sitting where you are, I want you to say the words "chicken fried sandwich". That's easy enough, a good conscious act. Now, try and think away pain. That doesn't work, does it? Oh, believe me, I've tried and it definitely doesn't work. Pain comes from the Subconscious You, to keep Conscious You safe. This is the message I want you to take from this chapter. The Conscious You controls how you interact with the environment around you and the Subconscious You takes care of everything else, which includes pain. As you move through life you'll create many outputs from your brain; happiness, sadness, excitement, love and anger to name just a few. These outputs are created based on how Subconscious You deals with the information (Input) that enters the brain and body. You are literally a little brain floating in a dark tank. You pull in information from the outside world via your nervous system, you process that information and then you make an output. Your subconscious has to sift through all of the information you are constantly receiving day in day out and it must decide what output to create that is in your best interest. We receive information into our brains from the world around us (Inputs). These could be sights, sounds, things you touch, observing an unfolding situation, watching a film, you name it. Any information that comes in is an input. It isn't the information coming in that creates the output, it is how that information is processed. To do this we use things like past experiences, beliefs, context, etc, to decide what output will be the best one for us to choose.

If you go and get a massage, the therapist will touch your skin. This is an input. You are in a dimly lit room and you know that for at least the next half hour, nothing really matters. Nobody is shouting MOM or DAD constantly, there is nothing to do but relax. Subconscious You will look at the context of the situation, it will see if there is any danger around, it will look at your current mood and it will use your past experience of the last time you had a massage. The Subconscious You, for most people in this situation, will create an output in the form of feel-good chemicals. Every single person reading this book is an individual. You are a person who feels and experiences the world around you in a way that is completely unique to you. Whilst people can experience the same input (say rock music), depending on how your brain processes that information, the output you get will vary. Some people may have fond memories of rock concerts in their youth and this can be a major factor that creates a feel-good output to listening to rock music. It is how we process information that is important, not so much the actual input. Hearing about a death in your immediate family will create a response which is unique to you. This output is dependent on multiple factors, including how you were feeling that day, how close you were to the deceased and your own beliefs about death. You may be more emotional than your brother or less so than your sister; everyone is different. The output (in this case grief) is based on how you process the input (hearing about the death) and pain is no different. Pain is an output 100% of the time. It changes depending on how you process the various inputs from the world.

How We Used to Think About Pain

There are literally no such things as pain receptors and to say otherwise is to trivialise the incredibly complicated nature of pain. There are zero nerves in your body that send information that you are in pain to your brain (that would be an input). There are many nerves that detect things like temperature, movement, vibration, chemicals, etc. But, there are no nerves that send pain signals. The closest things to pain receptors are nociceptors. Nociceptors are high threshold nerves that send information to the brain about potentially dangerous stimulus (think of when you stub your toe on a coffee table). It is up to Subconscious You to decide that the information (the input) coming into your brain (the blunt force trauma) warrants the response of creating pain (the output). Did you know that there a few people around the world who don't even feel pain? This is known as "congenital analgesia" and these guys and girls don't tend to live very long. How would you know if your appendix was about to burst if you couldn't feel pain? Or how would you know if you were walking on a fractured leg? Well, the truth is, if you had congenital analgesia, you wouldn't! Not experiencing pain doesn't work out very well for the human species. There's a reason we experience pain and it's not about damage. It's about protection. Pain science has come a long way since we first started to try to understand pain. Aristotle (384 BC – 322 BC) pushed that pain was caused by evil spirits entering the body during injury. Descartes (1596 – 1650) introduced and eventually solidified the Cartesian Model of Pain (CMP) into history and ultimately medical science. The CMP explained pain as being created in the tissues that would send pain signals to the brain. Even in 2018, a plethora of medical treatments are still being used based on the CMP where people receive nerve blocks, have nerves burnt or are given cortisone injections in attempt to relieve their pain. However, we now know this model, like many before, has pieces missing.

The Gate Control Theory (GCT) by Melzack and Wall was the next kid on the block. This theory explained how the spinal cord acted as gate keeper, choosing what dangerous and non-dangerous messages were sent to the brain. Even after some of the greatest minds had come together to help explain pain, the GCT could still not explain how people could be in pain without any messages being sent to the brain. Think of when amputees still feel pain in the limbs that they no longer have, or in our case much closer to home, when we feel pain despite the lack of tissue damage. If the GCT is to be believed, the pain we feel in these cases is not possible and we all know that's not true.

We then had the Neuromatrix Model of Pain followed and updated by the Cortical Body Matrix, which was heavily supported by evidence and built upon the principles of the formation of neurotags. But, alas, even in these later theories of pain, pieces were still missing.

Most recently, we have moved towards the Biopsychosocial (BPS) model of pain. This was first put forth by Dr George Engel in the 1970s. The Biopsychosocial model of pain considers all the biological, psychological and social factors which can influence pain. The Biopsychosocial model explains how pain is created and modulated by the brain, how pain can be influenced by tissue damage or created in the absence of tissue damage. It describes how pain is a multifactorial, personal experience. It is ultimately the BPS model of pain that helped me understand my own personal pain experience and help me ground my method in solid, evidence based science.

Pain is an Output

Mairi: Pain is an output? That came as a huge surprise to me. I would have always assumed that pain is an input. I thought that pain told me there's something wrong, that I was hurt or injured. Pain was there to tell me to stop doing what I was doing right then or to move away to somewhere safer to take the pain away. But Adam explained to me that it's an output which I create. I had studied pain as part of my first psychology degree and I knew that pain is a Biopsychosocial experience. The "bio" bit is how pain is experienced biologically, with nerve cells registering an impact or injury and sending a message to the brain that there could be a problem. The "psych" bit is what our brain does with this message, deciding how much suffering the physical threat should cause, both physical and emotional. The "social" bit is how it impacts on our daily life, via cultural and societal expectations and how, in turn, it determines how our lives affect the experience of our pain. For example, the culture you belong to will have an influence on your experience of pain, whether it's the stiff upper lip, big girls don't cry or no pain no gain mentality. All of these beliefs will make your pain experience different to someone from a different culture who might have different beliefs about pain. In the past, most beliefs around managing pain focussed on the "bio" bit, but that's only one part of the whole experience. The psychological and the social influences will also make a difference to how pain is felt. So, if any of the these BPS elements can change the experience of pain, I guess it's true: pain is an output!

Inputs and Outputs in Action

Adam: To see Inputs and Outputs in actions, let's take a look at an example;

Imagine Mairi is walking through the park one day. It's a beautiful day, the sun is shining, and the park is empty. Suddenly, a noisy dog crosses her path. Mairi receives the exact same information into her brain that I would receive had I also been in the park. Mairi's subconscious, in a blink of an eye, must decide what output is in her best, individual interest. The subconscious brain uses many things to decide on what output is an appropriate response and out of all the different factors involved, there are three we are most concerned about: context, belief and emotion. So, presented with the barking dog in front of her as an input into her brain, subconscious Mairi begins to assess the situation. Where is she? What is she doing? Who is she with? Has she been here before and if so, what happened last time? What does she know about the park? Is it safe? Are any emotions linked to this park? What does she know about dogs? Does she like dogs? What does it mean when a dog is barking loudly? To help answer these questions and decide on an output, subconscious Mairi pulls out what I call "the big book of life". In this book is every memory, feeling, belief and experience she has ever had. Everybody's brain has its own "big book of life" and it is essentially an encyclopaedia of you and your life. A quick flick through Mairi's big book of life and subconscious Mairi finds the memory of when she had been bitten by a dog when she was eight years old. Mairi keeps flicking and reads how the big scar she received that day has always made her self-conscious. Mairi reads about every other encounter she has had since the dog bite and remembers the feeling of anxiety that came with each experience. Subconscious Mairi takes a look around at the situation. The park is crowded, and she is alone. There isn't any other inherent danger around or anyone who could help her if she needed help. Mairi, based on the context of the situation, her own beliefs and emotions, creates a protection output that she thinks is most fitting based on her book of life. Her body is flooded with stress hormones like adrenaline and cortisol, her heart rate increases and the blood is drawn from her stomach and redirected to the largest of her muscles in preparation to make flight from or to fight this threat. She manages to slowly and carefully walk around the dog at a safe distance and continues on her way through the park. After a little while, Mairi's stress hormones diminish and she returns to how she felt before seeing the dog. She's unharmed, so her subconscious mind saves this information as the correct response procedure for the future, should she encounter a loudly barking dog again. This is going to be the first time I say this, but you are going to hear this a lot.... Everything you do either reinforces or breaks down a belief you hold.

This is an example of an input, the processing of the information contained in the input and an output being created. An Input can be considered any information that enters our Central Nervous System. This could be touch, smell, sight, sound or any situation that is composed of sensory information that reaches your spinal cord or brain. Somebody hands you a coffee, you smell something foul, you fall over, or you walk into new a room, these are all inputs. We are essentially brains floating in a dark tank, using our nervous system to feed information in. When we process the information, we create our own unique experience of the world around us. The protective output that Subconscious Mairi created, will help to cement Mairi's beliefs that barking dogs = danger and her behaviour to avoid contact with the noisy dog will help to protect her in the future.

If I had been walking through the park instead of Mairi and received the same input, I would have had a different output. My big book of life is far different to Mairi's so my view of what happened and how to respond would be different. I owned a small dog as a child and still, to this day, I love dogs. I would receive the same input, but because my book of life is slightly different (I have different beliefs and experiences) my subconscious would find no reason to create a negative output, as it wouldn't feel there was any danger. My output would be of feel-good chemicals, such as serotonin and oxytocin, which would help to cement my belief that dogs are not a threat and seeing a dog in the park is a pleasant and rewarding experience. However, If I was to be bitten by a dog next week, that experience may be enough to change my beliefs and begin to rewrite my book of life. The next time I see a dog, I might then be set on a different course of outputs. My big book of life is updated depending on the experiences I continue to encounter.

Mairi: In the science of psychology, this is called Schema Theory or heuristics. Although we believe that we only use a tiny fraction of our available brains, to cope with everyday living we need to make things as simple as possible to understand. If we took every input and analysed it for what it means, the possible impact, range of options on how to react etc., we wouldn't get out of bed in the morning. As we grow, we develop these little schemata (plural of schema) to provide mental shortcuts to help speed our progress through the world. We don't consciously need to think about our morning routine, for example. We just have a standard set of behaviours that we go through to present ourselves to the world, clean, fed, clothed and ready to take on what the day brings. The experience with the dog in the park is an example of a schemata. These will be listed and described in the big book of life that Adam refers to. Yet, they can be challenged and changed. This would happen if something changed unexpectedly. If Adam had been bitten one time, he might then be a bit more hesitant to approach a dog in future. If nothing bad happens in future, his original "dog encounter" schemata could be restored. If another unpleasant situation developed, however, he would add that information to his big book of life and maybe rewrite the schemata for the next time a dog passed his way. So, our experiences in life are always changing, and in turn how we expect to see the world will develop as life goes on.

Adam: So how do we apply this to pain? Well it's actually pretty easy. Pain is always an output and it comes under the Protection Output category that we will talk about in a moment. As you live and experience everything the world has to offer, you will create many different types of outputs. I classify outputs into five main groups: Protection, Belief Reinforcing, Mood, Subsidiary and Belief Dismantling outputs. If you can understand why certain inputs are processed in a way that creates a specific output, you can change how its processed and ultimately change the output.

What is Pain For?

You will set yourself on your path to recovery when you understand why we create each individual type of output and how they affect you as an individual. It's also important to realise that we often experience multiple types of outputs at the same time.

Mairi: Until I understood Adam's way of thinking about pain, I assumed that pain is pain and you just have to either numb it with medication or live with it. I had read the older medical theories of pain which talk about "pain receptors". I had also thought that how a person experiences pain is genetically hard wired. Some people have a high pain threshold, others not so much. The thing is, that doesn't really fit with my own experience. I've had four babies, three of which with no pain relief whatsoever. Yet when I was suffering with chronic pain, the slightest touch would cause an intense pain which can last all day. If my feelings of pain are genetically set, why would I be able to stand one really massive pain yet be reduced to tears by something that's really insignificant?

There is strong scientific evidence that challenges the idea that there is a "pain centre" in the brain, something that has always been assumed historically. To see the science behind this, have a look at the paper titled "Human brain mechanisms of pain perception regulation in health and disease" published by Dr. Vania Apkarian and colleagues in the European Journal of Pain in 2005. Modern neuroimaging studies have shown that different areas of the brain light up in parallel when pain is experienced. Some areas of the brain deal with the physical sensation that is being felt, deciding how sore the feeling is and whether is sharp, dull, hot, cold etc (the somatosensory areas). Other areas of the brain decide how the pain makes us feel. Are we scared, anxious, startled, depressed (the limbic system)? Then there's the issue of what the pain means to us (the prefrontal cortex). Does the pain mean we are in danger, is it something we need to pay attention to, is it the most important thing that's happening to us right now? All of these areas of the brain interact to decide what the person is experiencing and what it means to them. In other words, the brain decides what level of pain is being felt. This is clear support for Adam's understanding that pain is actually an output! Pain is determined and created by how our brains react to what we are experiencing. We create pain; it does not exist unless we make it happen, but it's not something which is done consciously.

How Chronic Pain is Processed

The modern studies of pain processing in the brain go on to show that the brains of people with chronic pain deal differently with pain processing compared to healthy people without medical conditions. The healthy people's systems deal with the experience mainly in the more primitive areas of the brain. Their brains focus on the somatosensory area to determine what the feeling is like and check the limbic system for memories of similar pain to see how they should respond. The brains of people with chronic pain have a different way of working, however. They tend to prioritise the signals in the prefrontal cortex, the area of the brain which deals with so-called executive functions. This means that the brains of people with chronic pain concentrate on the importance of the pain, what the consequences of it are, and how it affects what they are doing or plan to do. This isn't something people with chronic pain do deliberately, it's just the way their brains are wired. The focus goes to the executive functions rather than the basic sensations which just register that pain is being felt. The research can't say whether having this brain processing function means you're more likely to experience chronic pain, nor can it say that having chronic pain causes your brain to work this way. We only know that the two are linked. If we know that the brains of chronic pain sufferers work differently, though, we can do something about this. Once we now know what is happening, we can control our conscious thoughts to shift the subconscious processing of the pain output back to where it can be better managed. We need to understand the different outputs that are being produced and work out what we can do consciously to override our default subconscious position.

Protection Output

Adam: A Protection Output is where our subconscious self decides that, based on the inputs we know about, we need to protect ourselves from potential or actual danger or damage. Now, it's important to remember that what you deem as danger is going to be subjective. A good example of this is when you go to the emergency room. You sit down and within a few minutes your bum becomes numb, you start to feel stiff, lights seem brighter than normal and it definitely seems a lot colder. The nursing staff did not swap the chairs for incredibly uncomfortable ones in preparation for your arrival. The lights, chairs, and air temperature are all the same as you might come across in other places. As you walk into the emergency room, you receive an input from the environment. Subconscious You takes in all the information of the room and, upon checking in with your book of life, deems this place to be one of potential danger. Since you think this is somewhere you are potentially under threat, your senses heighten to make you more aware of your surroundings. Really think about it for a moment - what do you associate the emergency room with? Pain? Sickness? Boredom? The place where you received the bad news of "Well I'm sorry to say, you have fibromyalgia"? Or perhaps all of them? When it come to our big book of life, the emergency room has a pretty big section. It's a place you will have taken notice of. That's why Subconscious You gets ready to deal with something coming along that might cause you harm. However, if you look at most small children who have not spent much time in the same place, it is often a place of wonder. There are toys to play with, leaflets to throw about, all whilst their guardian sits there in pain. A Protection Output can cause you to feel may things, but it's the context of the situations that has the most power over what output is created as a Protection Output.

Creating pain isn't going to be a good idea on an eight-hour car journey, as it can distract you from driving and potentially...kill you. Creating stiffness however, is a brilliant way to force you to pull over and get out of the car to move around for ten minutes. Creating pain when faced with an aggressive wild animal isn't going to help the situation, but a release of adrenalin will. Pain is good way to protect you, but it isn't needed all of the time. Sometimes the feeling of anxiety can do the job much more effectively. However, if you dislocated your shoulder a year ago, you may find playing catch with your child will cause some niggles of pain. This isn't because it's still damaged, it's just a way of making you consciously aware of what you're doing with the arm you hurt. A few catching sessions later and Subconscious You might be happy that there is no danger playing catch and it never bothers you again.

Mairi: Feeling pain to protect yourself against future risk makes perfect sense. The very earliest philosophers understood that the brain would notice if you stuck your hand in a fire and would instruct your arm to pull the hand away from the flame, pronto! If you do something that causes you to hurt, your instincts tell you not to do that again. That's self-preservation and it's what we assume pain is for at its most basic level. For people with chronic pain, this processing in the brain seems to go into overdrive. (Giesecke et al., 2004; Seminowicz et al., 2006). This is especially true of people who have experienced something traumatic in their lives and who still bear the emotional scars. Exposure to trauma causes people to be more aware of risk and danger, a state we call hypervigilance. They are often, unknowingly, scanning the environment for potential threats. If they have been hurt before, they have solid evidence that danger exists. Our survival instincts then tell us to look out for danger in future to avoid bad things happening again. This hypervigilance to danger is reflected in the way that we deal with pain, making the experience even stronger and more important to us. In turn, this causes the brain to big up the importance of the threat and amplifies the pain we feel. This might explain why people who have experienced trauma are more likely to end up with fibromyalgia. Our brain becomes sharper on the detection of threats to avoid a repeat of a traumatic experience and in turn, it puts potential pain situations into sharper focus. We feel more pain, more often and at higher intensity. If we can be aware that this happens automatically in our brain, we can notice it happening and potentially break the automatic chain of events that leads to a severe and enduring pain experience.

Belief Reinforcing Output

Adam: A Belief Reinforcing Output is one where we consider what happened to us because of our reaction to experiences in our big book of life, to help the processing of inputs in the future. Our subconscious monitors what happened when we respond according to our previous experiences. It then uses any positive outcome to reinforce how we chose to act, if it helped. A good example of this is the story we just heard about Mairi and the dog in the park. After Mairi created a Protection Output, she managed to get around the dog without sustaining any personal damage. This will reinforce Mairi's belief that she should be wary around dogs as it has successfully protected her in the past. Always remember, it is far easier to reinforce a belief that it is to break it down, as us humans just don’t like to be wrong!

Mairi: This is so true! Psychologists call it confirmation bias and it's well known in all walks of life. They say that an interviewer makes up his opinion about a job candidate in the first thirty seconds. First impressions count! Time and time again psychological research has shown that once a decision has been made, people repeatedly look for evidence to confirm the decision. They often overlook potentially serious evidence that contradicts it, even when this evidence seems overwhelming. A study carried out in 2009 looked at people with political opinions and how they read information about key issues (Knobloch-Westerwick and Meng, 2009). The researchers watched how the people scanned the topics picking out only those they were interested in and reading only the material which supported their views. Although the research participants didn't know they were filtering out contradictory information and certainly didn't think they were doing this deliberately, subconsciously they only took in information which confirmed what they already thought. If you think about it, this makes sense to how we function in normal daily life. If we went through life weighing up the pros and cons of every belief we have and taking on board information that doesn't fit with our beliefs, we would very quickly be overwhelmed with doubts. We need to make a decision and stick to it in order to get through the basics of everyday living. This is how are brains are hardwired and we are not being stubborn or narrow minded in not accepting new ideas. It's a survival instinct, just as strong as avoiding danger and learning from experience. Sometimes, though, information comes to light which just cannot be ignored.

When the misbehaviour of a much beloved celebrity is reported it's so hard to believe that they could do such a thing. We've come to think we know someone and then they do something that's completely out of character. At first, we don't believe it and might point to all the charity support or photo calls with puppies that we've seen. But gradually, the evidence builds and reluctantly we begin to believe that there is substance in the new information that has come to light. Changing our mind about something can be very difficult, with our brains resisting and challenging the process at every stage. We call this situation cognitive dissonance and it's one that psychologists have known about since the earliest days of cognitive science (Festinger, 1956). Cognitive dissonance is a really uncomfortable state to be in. We might experience it as guilt, anger, frustration, embarrassment, anxiety, dread etc. When we hold two opposing beliefs at the same time, our brain bounces back and forward between the two and this situation doesn't feel good at all. We try to avoid being in this state and will go a long way to do so. We might have seen evidence that something we do is not good for our health. In my case, it's sugar based. Show me a box of doughnuts and I'll show you an empty box. I know that taking in too many calories will cause me to put on weight, stop me eating healthier options containing nutrients and fibre and probably cause me to crash in exhaustion on the sofa once the sugar rush wears off. And yet, I find myself buying and eating sugar based treats regularly. Afterwards I feel guilty, ashamed and lacking self-discipline. This is cognitive dissonance. To resolve the conflict I feel with myself, I have three choices. I can change how much value I give to the conflicting belief, in this case that the sugar is unhealthy. I might say that, yes, the cake contains sugar and white flour but it was produced organically so it really can't be bad for me. I might start to focus on a new belief that supports my behaviour. If I eat all of these high calorie treats I'll have lots of energy and be able to go out and do some healthy exercise. Or of course, I could change the behaviour altogether. Stop eating the doughnuts. Euch. Any of these three options would remove the state of cognitive dissonance and stop me feeling uncomfortable about the behaviour. What's important, though, is to know what it is that's making me feel uncomfortable (that I have two beliefs that contradict each other) and try to find a way to sort the situation out.

Mood Output

Adam: A Mood Output is when Subconscious You deems that, due to the input you are receiving, a change in mood is in our best interest. The Mood Output is a good one to start to change how you think of pain. When you are hungry, the feeling doesn't come from your stomach, it comes from your brain. When you are sexually aroused the feeling doesn't come from your groin, it comes from your brain. When you feel sad, the sadness doesn't come from your heart, it comes from your brain. How you feel day to day is always an output. So, it follows that when you are in pain, it doesn't come from the tissue, it comes from the brain. Mood outputs help us respond to the state of the world in a timely manner. If we are with a group of people who are enjoying a laugh and a joke, we will change our mood to a more pleasant one to help cement us socially. Remember, we are all social animals at heart. Moods such as anger and fear are essential as they help avoid or deal with potentially dangerous situations. There is even some emerging research that shows that being in a bad mood can actually benefit us as it makes us more focused in a difficult situation. A good example of a Mood Output would be when you sit down to have your favourite meal in your favourite restaurant. You've anticipated something lovey, but on this occasion, the food just doesn't taste as good as you expected. You instantly become disappointed and your mood changes. The feel-good chemicals you had been anticipating didn't appear and instead your mood becomes negative. This should prompt us to do something to recover our previous positive state. What we should do is complain and tell the restaurant staff that we are unhappy with the meal. This gives them a chance to put the situation right and perhaps bring us something else which is up to the usual high standard they serve. What often happens is that we say nothing and leave unhappy, vowing never to return. If we pay attention to our mood and respond to negative changes, we are responding appropriately to the negative Mood Output we have created.

Mairi: Being in constant severe pain has definitely affected my mood over the years. I was depressed and anxious because I couldn't do what I needed or wanted to do and worried that my family were suffering as a result. I was also angry that the years were passing me by and that I was getting worse over time, not better. Now I understand this was because I was reinforcing my belief that the pain was caused by physical damage or that something was wrong with me. However, by moving less, I was causing myself more pain, not less. By far, the mood that my pain was reinforcing most strongly was fear. I was terrified to move too much or to push myself too far in case it caused a flare up of symptoms. It's true that sometimes overdoing things would cause more pain but this was probably due to my deconditioning more than anything else! When I did move more it makes sense that my muscles would feel that they had been worked. Unfortunately, my subconscious brain was misinterpreting this as potential damage and was creating a pain output to stop this happening again! One I realised that I was misinterpreting movement as pain, I could break the cycle and start to move more during the day. The pain got less once I started to accept that I was not causing myself damage. Over time, my level of movement in a normal day has increased significantly and my pain levels have reduced to zero.

Subsidiary Output

Adam: A Subsidiary Output is where our subconscious decides, based on various inputs, that it is safe enough to focus on bodily functions, feel good chemicals and emotions that we do not need initially to stay alive in the face of danger. A good example of this is when we have a big Sunday dinner, begin to feel tired and decide to go relax on the sofa. Subconscious You takes a look at the situation and realises that we are nice and safe in our home. Since we believe it's safe to do so, our body then begins to digest the food we had eaten for dinner. It's important to note that we cannot produce a Subsidiary Output if we are producing a Protection Output. Subsidiary Outputs create happy hormones and neurotransmitters that make us feel good. They initiate digestion and a switch of body modes into anabolic (building cells). Subsidiary Outputs allow us to be happy, to rest, and to digest. Imagine if a huge bear walked into the room whilst you are reading this book and when you were nice and relaxed. To respond with fight or flight in response to the present danger (the bear) you need stress hormones, you need the blood from your stomach to be diverted to your largest muscles for extra energy. This will maximise your chances of survival. Digesting the bagel you had this morning, growing your finger nails or simply feeling content, are all Subsidiary Outputs that will not help us survive, so the Protection Output overrides the Subsidiary Output.

Mairi: Everything that our bodies do, whether consciously or subconsciously, is controlled by a crucial structure within us: our nervous system. It is formed by two parts. The Central Nervous System is the name given to the brain and spinal cord working together. The Peripheral Nervous System is mainly made up of nerves and it's this system that connects the Central Nervous System to the rest of our body. Within the Peripheral Nervous System, we have a Somatic Nervous System which controls the movements that we choose to make and the Autonomic Nervous System which sorts out what goes on inside the body. There's another level with the Autonomic Nervous System (ANS) where two different systems control what's going on internally. The Sympathetic Nervous System (SNS) is like our action force that jumps into gear and sorts out what happens when we need to respond to an emergency situation. It makes energy for us to take on whatever threat we have perceived and gets our bodies ready to respond. The Parasympathetic Nervous System (PNS) is the other side of the coin. It helps to slow our heart rate to allow us to relax, it diverts blood to our digestive systems to allow us to process food that we've consumed. It's the "rest and digest" alternative to the Sympathetic Nervous System's "fight or flight" responses. The SNS is the accelerator for our bodies; the PNS is effectively the brake.

Adam's description of Subsidiary Outputs is an explanation of this PNS at work. We need both the SNS and PNS to control how we react to the experiences that our Peripheral Nervous System picks up. The resources that our bodies have available are limited and our clever Autonomic Nervous System decides whether they are best used to protect us against a perceived threat or whether we can use them to take on board more fuel for later use, for example. We can't do both at the same time and it's more important for our survival to deal with an immediate threat than to get ready to challenge threats that may come along in future. That's why the Protection Output that we create will always override the Subsidiary Output. In the short term, that's the correct decision, but we need the PNS to be activated for long term survival. The perfect balance of the two is called homeostasis, which is what our nervous system is always trying to achieve. There has to be sufficient energy allocated to the PNS to allow us to stay strong and fit in the long term, to be ready for when our SNS needs to kick in for survival.

Belief Dismantling Output

Adam: A Belief Dismantling Output is where Subconscious You decides that creating doubt or dismantling a belief is in our best interest as a result of an input being received. A good example of this is the "why did the chicken cross the road" joke we discussed earlier. Your understanding of that joke was based on an earlier version of yourself, a version with limited knowledge of the world around you. Presented with new information that give different context, Subconscious You easily began to break down your old belief of that joke. There is something I want to point out here. The breaking down of a joke you didn't fully understand, is fairly easy. After all, it makes no real difference to you if you hadn't fully understood it. Dismantling your beliefs on pain however, is far harder, as it's something very personal to us. Beliefs that are personal to us require a lot of work to dismantle!

Mairi: From a psychological perspective, dismantling your existing beliefs is one of the hardest things you can attempt to do. We are designed to learn from our experiences, make sense of them and move forward in the understanding that our belief is correct. Working out how to challenge what we believe and change our personal opinions has been the holy grail of psychology from the very beginning. Marketing professionals build a career on encouraging us to form new opinions, politicians try to make us believe that they know how we should be living our lives and hope to get us to support their manifestos and healthcare professionals will often need us to develop a different way of thinking about things in order to improve our physical and mental health. Whilst these and many other professions have spent decades studying how we form beliefs and how we can be persuaded to change them, this science is definitely a work in progress. What we know so far can help you prepare for the shift in beliefs that is likely to be needed to challenge the way you manage your chronic pain.

In the section on Belief Reinforcing, we introduced the idea of cognitive dissonance. This is where there is a conflict between different thoughts that we have. For example, we may believe that smoking is a positive experience for us, but we also know that there is a strong link between smoking and cancer. This leads us to enjoy an experience which we believe is damaging us. We might believe that our chances of personally developing cancer are low or that the cancer research is flawed and this could help reduce the uncomfortable feeling of dissonance. If new information comes to light, perhaps a close relative developing cancer or further information produced by researchers becomes available, this can strengthen the position of harm that we attribute to smoking. Our dissonance then becomes magnified, and this is the time that we are often motivated to act to reduce these upsetting feelings.

When we are faced with compelling evidence that challenges our existing beliefs, we can find ourselves concluding that we may need to adjust our understanding. If the evidence is strong or the issue is particularly important to us, we evaluate what we know now and decide to alter our beliefs in some way. Sometimes, this can be a fairly straightforward choice, such as the real meaning of Adam's chicken story. Once we understand that the story is about a suicidal chicken, we can probably accept this new meaning and perhaps smile ruefully at the twist in the meaning that we hadn't previously been aware of. When it comes to something that's personally important to us, the change in belief is not quite so straightforward. Throughout this book, your existing beliefs about the diagnosis of fibromyalgia and how our brain processes pain are likely to be challenged. This will be difficult to deal with, especially if you've been living with the diagnosis for some time. Your life will have changed as a result of living with chronic pain and you will have made lots of adjustments to help you cope and get through each day. Changing your fundamental beliefs about pain will need you to make more changes in your life, often going against decisions that you made previously. You have new information now and that information can help your brain to produce the Belief Dismantling Output that is needed to take control of your life and be free of pain. It's not easy, but it can be done.

Sometimes, the opinion of someone you know can influence your choices and this is especially true when you are challenging important beliefs. If you have someone close to you who supports your desire to change, they can be the catalyst to really helping you break free of pain. An unhelpful opinion or unkind comment that encourages you to doubt the new information you have can be a significant setback, however. Later in the book we talk about support groups and their potential influence on people who are trying to rid themselves of the fibromyalgia diagnosis. If you're reading this book, you have probably taken the decision that you want to improve your health and that you are open to new ideas that can help you to do that. Not everyone who suffers the same symptoms is in that place at the same time as you, and when you start to challenge your core beliefs, you are essentially challenging their core beliefs too. If they are not ready to hear about this, or don't have the same background information as you, they are like the smoker who isn't ready to give up yet. Their way of resolving their cognitive dissonance can be to discredit your information and declare it to be untrue. The information we have provided in this book comes from credible scientific sources and personal experience of people known to Adam and myself but people who don't read the book or who are not ready to receive new information will not accept this. Unfortunately, you have to allow them to resolve their dissonance as they see fit. Be aware of this and don't let their resolution of some uncomfortable feelings set you back on your road to recovery.

Getting Stuck in Protection Output Mode

Mairi: When you have experienced chronic pain, your brain seems to prioritise protection above all else in terms of the output to choose. If there is any risk to you, then of course this has to be the priority that you deal with. The problem with your chronic pain brain is that you get stuck in the Protection Output mode, often incorrectly interpreting the pain you feel as being a threat to you. You are also generating a strong Belief Reinforcing Output to maintain your level of chronic pain as a continuing threat and one which tells you to stop doing anything that might be maintaining the pain. Your brain is reinforcing the incorrect belief that the pain you are feeling is from damage. Your medical team will have confirmed that this is not necessarily true. If you have no disease or tissue damage that is worsened by movement, the pain you feel as a Protection Output and a Belief Reinforcing Output is maladaptive – it is doing you more harm than good. However, your brain feels it is in your best interest to incapacitate you with pain to keep you safe. Movement in everyday life is not what is causing the pain. You have felt some pain in the past and your brain has decided that you need to be protected from more pain. It then produces pain which you do not need to make you avoid any activity that might be a threat in future. This continues in a loop with the level of sensitivity to perceived threat increasing on each cycle. Ultimately, your brain is trying to protect you from a threat that doesn't exist, but that you believe must exist, when you only know that pain can be felt when damage is present. Your Belief Reinforcing Output has generated a Protection Output to protect you from a threat that doesn't exist. In doing so it is limiting your level of movement and causing you further harm.

It's not just Adam that believes this is the case! Dr Katja Wiech from the University of Oxford published an important article in a prestigious academic journal called "Trends in Cognitive Science" in 2008. The research showed that pain is amplified by the attention we give it, because we believe it may cause us harm. In fact, this is not the case. The pain that you are feeling is not warning you of harm, it is causing harm! We will work on changing this process within this book, using your new knowledge to challenge this unhelpful belief and changing this thought process.

Using Inputs and Outputs to Understand Pain

The Impact of Previous Knowledge

Adam: Once you understand how people can experience the same inputs, yet can experience completely different outputs, it brings you one step closer to recovery. As you go about your daily life you will see inputs everywhere. You will see them as a group of friends laughing at a joke, whilst one of the friends doesn't quite understand the joke and because of this, doesn't laugh (a different output from their friends). You will see different inputs and outputs when couples view art at a gallery and one person loves an artwork whilst the other hates it. The more you can understand that it's not the input that is important, but how we process the input, then the easier it is to start your recovery.

A popular advertising campaign a few years back for the Skoda car company played on people's memories of how bad Skoda cars were considered in years previous. The whole marketing campaign had the tagline, "It's a Skoda, honest! ". Let's take the example above and imagine several people of different ages standing at a bus stop. The people at the bus stop are all looking up at a bill board with the tag, "It's a Skoda, honest!". The individuals who were around during the time when Skoda was considered a terrible model of car will understand this joke. However, any younger people who were children around this time will not understand this joke. That is, unless, they are told the piece of information which is vital to understanding the joke, i.e. that Skoda was considered a terrible make of car years ago. If you were to tell the young person, “Hey, Skoda used to be notorious for making bad cars” then with the additional information they now have, they can subconsciously process the input of the billboard and assign new meaning to it, thus creating a different output. This is a good example of how different outputs can be created based on many factors, in this instance, age.

Making Sense of What We Encounter

The human brain constantly works to make sense of the world around us and you will find, as a species, we have a tendency and a desire to label everything. We segment things to better understand them and most of all, we use the past to give meaning to the present.

Our subconscious is constantly using inputs, beliefs, past experiences, emotions and everything else, to give meaning to what we see, feel and ultimately, experience. Over the years we get so good at filling in the blanks that we can sometimes see things that are not really there. Have you every woken up in the middle of the night, in a dark room, and noticed the shape of a person in the corner of the room, only for it to turn out to be a dressing gown? Perhaps sometimes when you look at certain patterns you can see faces in them?

If you look at the picture above, you will see it's a picture of white and black blobs. But, what does this picture mean to you? Can you see a face in it? Or perhaps you may see an object? Your brain right now, is trying to make sense of this picture (the input), using your memories, your beliefs (perhaps it looks like something you have seen before) and everything else and is desperately trying to associate meaning to the picture. However, no matter how long you look at this picture, your output is going to remain the same. This is unless, you have new information to help process the picture differently. If you look at the following picture, you will get this new information.

Now that you have new information, in the form of the second picture, even though you are receiving the same input from the original picture (looking at the first picture), this new information allows you to process it differently and to create a new output in terms of seeing something in the picture that you couldn't previously. The input remains the same, but you can now see what the picture is of because of new information. This information will get stored in your book of life and the next time you see this picture, you will automatically know what it is. This is a good example of how snippets of information that we are told, that we read or are shown, can create completely different "new" outputs. So, I want you to really think about how simple pieces of information can negatively affect you. Imagine a doctor tells you that you have a slipped a disc (remember it is impossible to slip a disc. You can bulge them, but they don't slip), think about how having this piece of "wrong" information can affect you! The next time you go to pick something up, Subconscious You will remember when they refer to the book of life and they are going to make a different output because of this new information, whether it's true or not. Now, this output could be in the form of fear of movement, it could be pain, or it could be your back feeling stiff to force you to protect it. Inputs and outputs are everywhere and everything you are told, feel, believe and experience can create different outputs and sometimes these are not for the best.

A long time ago you could sit and enjoy a good film at the local cinema. You could sit for two straight hours in the same position, all whilst never moving a muscle. You could eat popcorn with your neck extended right back while staring up at the big screen. You would be thoroughly engaged in the tantalising movements of Patrick Swayze during "Dirty Dancing" and you could enjoy an enriching social activity with friends, family or a loved one. However, if your reading this book, I'm going to guess that it's been a while since you have done that. These days it's going to go more so along the lines of, that you get into the cinema and after ten minutes you become so uncomfortable that you must leave. Because of physical pain, you have had to forgo a social activity, which means it's also going to affect your psychological health. Whether it's the biological that affects the psychological, or it's the social that affects the physical, one this is certain, they all interact and influence each other.

In the cinema example above, the input of watching the film has remained pretty much unchanged over the years. In fact, cinema chairs are now made bigger and more comfortable than they were twenty years ago, and the screens are also likely to be larger. So, in actual fact, the whole cinema experience is now designed to be more comfortable than ever before. However, despite this, those in pain can't attend as they find it far too painful. As you will read a lot in this book "It's not the input that matters, it's the processing" and this is so true in the cinema example. The cinema, or in fact any activity that now causes you pain where it previously didn't, is an example of how it is not the inputs that matter when we are in chronic pain, but the processing. Despite all the doom and gloom there is still hope, there is still a way out of it and you can thank being plastic for that.... Which is what the next chapter is about.

Mairi: I remember telling a friend what it's like to live with fibromyalgia. For me, there was a constant aching in my arms and legs. My arms were the worst which meant that any walking aids were no use to me. Although I described it as an ache it was very painful, but more like a crushing feeling than a sharp pain, usually. Along with this, I had "fireworks" going off randomly round my body. These were sharp stabs, like an electric shock, that would keep me awake at night and cause spasms and stress during the day. Strong painkillers usually took the edge off the pain and meant I could move but I wouldn't be able to get out of bed in the morning until I'd taken my first dose and the analgesia had kicked in. I took four doses of meds during the day so the pain levels cycled up and down as the painkillers took effect and wore off. Sometimes the pain was too intense to move at all and I would be in tears with the severity of it. On these days I would resort to morphine and just hope that it passed soon. Usually two or three days later it had eased enough to go back to the usual painkiller dose. The pain was never not there. Along with the pain came crippling fatigue. Not just feeling tired, feeling totally immobilised. Exhausted. No energy for movement at all. On a good day I could walk the length of an aisle in the supermarket and back, but that would be about all. By the time I reached the checkout I would be in severe pain and completely drained. My children helped by getting the shopping for me and carrying it. I would sit down while they packed the bags to save enough energy to get back to the car. Covering any distance needed a wheelchair. On my wedding day, I reached the venue for the event by wheelchair. I walked the few steps down the wedding aisle but had to sit down for the whole ceremony. Not exactly the dream wedding I had imagined.

So how do you cope with something like this? Especially when you've been told that doctors don't know what causes it, that there is no treatment and that there is definitely no cure? That's a very difficult question to answer, but I know I tried every idea I could find. I swallowed countless dietary supplements which I'd been told would make a difference. And this happened at enormous expense I might add! I already had a cocktail of tablets to take every day and some days just being able to get them down was difficult. Occasionally I thought I detected an improvement but after a few days, the pain and fatigue would be as bad as ever. I tried heat treatments, cold treatments, electrical treatments, meditation, journaling, everything I could possibly find. Sometimes it appeared that things were getting better but sooner or later, the situation returned to the normal pain, fatigue and confusion that identifies fibromyalgia. Scientific researchers have identified ways of identifying coping styles and strategies and grouping these into broad categories. They usually measure them using questionnaires and this helps identify what people actually do to cope with situations in life. It also helps to identify what types of coping are most helpful in terms of positive outcomes and symptom reduction.

How You Cope Affects How You Cope

Different types of coping can be used for different experiences. We can try to think that a situation is not as bad as it seems, we can think that it could be worse and know that other people have had more serious conditions to deal with. We can distract ourselves and try to keep our minds occupied, get angry, make jokes about it, the list goes on and on. The one thing that keeps coming out of the studies that have been carried out is that thinking about how awful the pain feels definitely makes it worse. Not only does it increase the impact of the pain, but it actually affects how our brains process pain. Our thoughts change the way our brains deal with the pain, biologically intensifying the experience. We are, effectively, manufacturing our own pain by how we think about it!

A group of doctors and researchers from Michigan, USA investigated this idea using functional Magnetic Resonance

Imaging (MRI scans) (Gracely, Geisser, Giesecke, Grant, Petzke, Williams & Clauw, 2004). The participants in the study had been diagnosed with fibromyalgia and were checked to make sure they didn't have anything that might have influenced the testing like other medical conditions, substance use or excess caffeine intake or smoking. Under close medical supervision, they stopped taking medications which might have affected the results and they were evaluated, monitored and scanned over a two-day period. They were also tested for their level of pain sensitivity by having increasing levels of weights applied to their thumbs, squeezing them hard to make them feel higher levels of pain. Who volunteers to do this, seriously? But this gave a good measure of how the people reacted to the same levels of pain, meaning that direct comparisons could take place between the different people's responses to the same levels of measured pain. Overwhelmingly, the thing that made the pain experience worse was thinking about how horrible it was and focussing on the negativity of the experience. Having more pressure applied to their thumbs, being depressed about the situation or how much the pain affected their lives was not the key thing that made a difference. It was all to do with what people thought about the pain rather than the pain itself. In addition, thinking negatively about the pain made the fear of pain increase. The areas of the brain which deal with fear were activated more often and more intensely in people who dwelled on the awfulness of the experience. The brains in these people responded more easily to the fear and this, in turn, led to brain activity which continued and intensified the feelings of fear. The brain then responded to this fear of pain by activating the areas that deal with attention and emotions about pain and stimulated these areas. This led to a "brain behaviour" in the people who thought more negatively about the pain, meaning they felt more pain, more often and for longer than people who didn't focus so much on the awfulness of their situation. A whole unique vicious cycle had been set up in the brains of catastrophizers, making the pain experience so much worse!

People who were more negative about their pain experience had higher levels of fear and anticipation of more pain. Their brains were then more sensitive to the squeezing of their thumbs and they felt more pain. Afterwards, their brains stayed activated to remind them that the pain had been so bad and to keep them alerted to the fact that more pain might be just around the corner. So, the brains of this group of people had set up a process to make their pain worse, last longer and appear more easily than people who didn't dwell on how bad their experience was! The brain is an amazing computer, it's true, but sometimes it can be our own worst enemy! It can actually intensify pain and make us suffer more than we need to.

Other researchers in Edinburgh have reported that how we think about pain affects the level of impact it has on our daily functioning. This group studies people experiencing chronic pain and found that the level of pain was not the main factor influence on quality of life. Thinking about how bad the condition was and believing it would have more of a negative impact in the future seems to make the impact of the condition worse, even in people who didn't rate their pain as to be as severe as people who didn't have these views. So, it wasn't the level of pain that made the condition worse, it was how people thought about it! It makes sense, then, that changing how you think about your condition can make it more tolerable and lead to a better quality of life. Hopefully, reading this book will help you do just that.

Again, as a scientist. I'm naturally cautious about accepting the results of the research and making sense of them. It seems likely that people who think their symptoms have more impact on their lives would be suffering more. That's a chicken and egg conversation! What's interesting from this research is that the level of pain being experienced wasn't the main thing that impacted on people's lives. I would have assumed that being in more pain is worse than experiencing a little pain and therefore people in more pain would say that their lives were affected more. But this isn't what these researchers found. People who said they had lower levels of pain could have a worse experience if they worried about their pain and thought it wasn't going to improve. But how are these linked? Which comes first; does worrying about the pain make it have more impact or does pain that has more impact cause a higher level of worry? This question was addressed by researchers in Switzerland who followed a group of chronic pain patients over time. By measuring pain, level of disability, mood and thoughts about their condition over six months, the researchers were able to identify the direction of cause and effect. The main predictor of the outcome for patients was believing that the pain would have serious consequences on a person's life. More than the level of pain being experienced, more than being depressed or anxious, believing that pain would be worse determined whether or not the pain actually did worsen over time. A number of studies support these findings. How you feel about the pain you are experiencing and how much of a problem it causes you will make a difference in the quality of your life.

The good news is, we can break this cycle and make our brains reduce our pain experience. Regardless of how much pain we are feeling, we can stop our brains from automatically seeking out pain, from actively looking for opportunities to hurt. We can reduce how much pain we feel and how much it affects us. We can stop the pain experience from lasting so long. Effectively, we can "cure" ourselves of this horrible condition.

What About the Other Symptoms of Fibro?

The Spoon Theory

Mairi: Fibromyalgia is not just about the pain. If you've had fibromyalgia for a while you will no doubt have heard the story of the spoons. In summary, the spoon theory explains that energy is limited (this is the number of spoons a person has in a day) and what you can do in a day has to be carefully chosen because of the limit of energy available (spend your spoons wisely). When I had fibro, I thought this was the perfect explanation for how I managed my days. The medical profession had repeatedly stressed the importance of pacing, not taking on too much and ending up being exhausted and definitely stopping any activity that caused pain. Respectfully, I now believe that this approach was counterproductive and actually made the pain and fatigue I was experiencing worse and don't even get Adam started on pacing!

A typical day would go something like this: I need to get up, get washed and dressed. I've got kids to get out to school and dinner to prepare for their return. If I have any energy left over, the dog could do with a walk. My alarm goes off and it's time to get up. I don't feel refreshed after a night's sleep, in fact I'm pretty much exhausted and every muscle in my body seems to be burning. It feels like I ran a marathon yesterday, and getting out of bed takes a while. I take my first dose of painkillers and wait for them to kick in while encouraging the children to leave for school. I'm too sore to shower so I run a bath. The effort to get upstairs to the bathroom floors me so I lie on my bed while the bath fills. The warmth of the water feels good and this, combined with the effect of the painkillers, reduces my pain enough to help me get dressed. This soon drains my reserves again so I struggle carefully downstairs and sit for a while to let the pain recede a bit and to summon the energy for the next thing on my list. Soon it's lunchtime but I'm not really hungry. I should eat something to try to top up my energy reserves so I grab tea and biscuits, maybe a sandwich if there's something suitable in the fridge. I'm upset to realise that the effort of this has floored me again. Time for my second dose of meds for the day. I'm so exhausted I can hardly keep my eyes open and I drift into deep sleep. I'm woken by the kids returning from school and though I feel as though I've been out cold, I'm not refreshed and don't feel any better about the sleep. I look for something to make for dinner. Preparation has to be kept to a minimum as my hands ache and my arms are throbbing in pain. I'm not good with knives as the scars on my fingers will confirm, my grip just wasn't strong enough. Something simple from the freezer will have to do. I set the timer and sit down again, exhausted by the effort of the transfer from freezer to oven. When the timer sounds, I struggle back to the kitchen and reach for the plates from the cupboard. The pain in lifting these means I can do only one at a time. My third dose of painkillers will hopefully make the pain recede a little. The smell of the dinner starting to char in the oven reminds me that although I switched the timer off, I didn't remember to take the food out of the oven or to switch the oven off.

Still sore, still tired, it's time for the final dose of pain relief of the day. I hope that this will be enough to get me some sleep. I'll wake a couple of times in the night to go to the loo but so long as it's not a night of total insomnia (which happened a lot) I should be ok to get the kids off to school the next day.

What a life. No life at all. Looking back at the typical day now, there is hardly any movement happening. Moving less causes muscles to become deconditioned and guess what? Pain and fatigue get worse. The term that scientists have used for the last thirty plus years to describe this is The Disuse Syndrome (Bortz, 1984). Humans are designed to move. Thinking back to the caveman days, we were either hunting down dinner or running away from predators. Sitting down all day was just not an option. You'd be eaten for sure. So, our bodies are designed to move, not to lie in bed or sit at a desk for hours on end. This sedentary lifestyle makes our health worse. It's no surprise that lack of movement causes deconditioning, making movement more painful and more tiring, but did you know how much it also affects other functions in the body?

Fibro Fog

For me, the fibro fog was actually the worst symptom of fibromyalgia. My concentration and memory were seriously affected. When tested by my GP, their functioning was at the same level as someone with moderate dementia. At one point, I was even tested for early onset dementia, as the mistakes I was making and things I was forgetting were starting to become dangerous. Of course, the drugs I was taking for pain relief had a variety of side effects which included fatigue, memory disturbance and the potential to affect my concentration. The warning not to drive or operate machinery was widespread, and I certainly did avoid driving unless it was essential. But this isn't the full picture. A systematic review of published research into the link between lack of movement and brain functioning was published in 2017 in the British Journal of Sports Medicine by Dr Ryan Falck and colleagues. The review was carried to find out more about how dementia symptoms might be affected by taking exercise. The results strongly showed that memory function and concentration decline when movement reduces. Moving more reversed the decline and improved brain function overall. For a clinical explanation see the research paper titled "Lipid metabolism in cognitive decline and dementia" published by Professor Francesco Panza in 2006 in the academic journal "Brain Research Reviews". This paper can explain the biochemical interactions that happen and the science behind the changes in the brain. The good news from the Falck et al review is that increasing the amount of movement will help memory and concentration improve. Let's be clear here, the researchers are not claiming that exercise can cure dementia! The evidence does exist to show that moving more will reduce the risk of developing dementia. For fibromyalgia sufferers, getting active will help clear the fibro fog. Getting off the pain killers will help even more.

Sleep

To sleep, perchance to dream. Perchance would be a fine thing! How frustrating is it when you're exhausted, can hardly keep your eyes open and yet you can't get any sleep at all? Sleep disturbance is a common symptom in fibromyalgia as you probably know. When your sleep is disturbed, the way your brain processes pain is affected. You feel pain more easily and at a higher intensity, so if you're already suffering with pain and this keeps you awake, you will then experience more pain and another vicious circle begins. Because we're more tired and in more pain, we probably move less. Multiple studies have been carried out which show that increasing the amount of movement we have during a day would help us sleep better, which makes perfect sense. If were physically tired after exertion surely sleep will be easier? Some researchers have used healthy volunteers to investigate the impact of sleep deprivation on pain. Research by Schuh-Hofer and colleagues in 2013 showed that, even after one night of sleeplessness, the healthy volunteers reported higher levels of pain. When the healthy participants were people who took a lot of exercise, however, the sleep deprivation did not lead to increases in pain. So, the evidence suggests that moving more will help us sleep better, which in turn will reduce pain, which will help encourage us to move more. The vicious circle can become a virtuous circle when you move more.

Bowels

Let's touch on the delicate topic of bowel movements. Constipation can be a problem for people with fibromyalgia, and

Irritable Bowel Syndrome (IBS) is a common co-existing condition. Scientists have studied the factors which are associated with digestive problems and how they are affected by lack of movement and exercise. Regardless of whether people have enough fibre in their diet, people who don't move much during the day are more likely to find themselves having trips to the bathroom less often. If constipation has become an issue, it will almost certainly be made worse by the painkillers that chronic pain sufferers take. So, laxatives are required, and another vicious circle begins. Researchers have found that IBS symptoms, including constipation, can be relieved by increasing the amount of moving around you do in a day (see Daley et al., 2008 for evidence). The hormones which are needed to help our digestive system function efficiently are stimulated when we get moving (for a full explanation see de Oliveira & Burini, 2009) but it's fair to say that regular movement helps regulate bowel movements! Saving your spoons is therefore likely to make your digestive system problems worse, adding to the misery of the experience that is fibromyalgia.

Itching

Itching, particularly late at night, is another very distressing symptom of fibromyalgia. Even talking about itching makes me itchy. But just like the other fibro symptoms, it's definitely not something that you are imagining! In some people, the itching can even be accompanied by a rash, visual proof that there's something really unpleasant going on in the skin. Itchiness is a function of the nociceptor pathways, which we know already are involved in pain detection so it's perhaps not surprising that the system is also causing problems with itching. Some medications have itchiness as a side effect but some of the medication for itching like antihistamines can in turn cause drowsiness. This is another vicious circle of symptoms and medications to contend with in fibromyalgia where the medications can sometimes add to the problems. You have to make a decision on which symptom is worse for you and whether it's worth tolerating the side effect to reduce the impact of the initial problem. I've found that the other nasty symptoms of fibromyalgia have pretty much disappeared along with the pain, since I changed the way I thought about my condition and followed Adam's advice to just move more!

Being Plastic

Bioplasticity in Action

Adam: Your body, my body, pretty much everybody's body is plastic. And I don't mean you're a Barbie or a Ken doll kind of plastic. The plastic I'm talking about, well we call that Bioplasticity!

Bioplasticity refers to the ability of our bodies, not just our brains, to adapt to the demands forced upon them. If you play guitar for an hour every day, you will soon find that the skin on the fingers you press on the strings to make chords with will grow hard and thicker, allowing you to play longer and better! If you are exposed to a certain type of bacterium your immune system will become better adapted to fighting it next time you come across it. When you walk into a dark room your pupils will dilate to allow more light in, making you able to see more effectively. We are in every sense of the word...adaptable. This plasticity has come in handy throughout our evolution and has ultimately lead us to this point in time, where compared to 50,000 years ago, we are very, very comfortable. Bioplasticity has definitely worked for us and still continues to do so, just think of when you want to learn a new instrument. However, it can and will work against us.

The simple fact is, because you are plastic, whatever you do you will get better at. We adapt well to everything. So, when we start creating pain, when we really don't need to, bioplasticity jumps at the chance to help! The longer you are in pain, the better you get at making it. In the same way your fingers adapt and grow callouses for guitar playing, so does your brain and nervous system for protection. Over time the brain and nervous system can almost get rewired for pain, so to speak. Imagine you have to walk home every day from the shops and to get home you must pass through a dark alleyway. Now you have done this trip a hundred times and every time it has been completely fine. However, one day you get mugged. You are obviously upset, but luckily you are unharmed.

Now let's say a week goes by and this is the first time you have had to do this trip again. As soon as you get close to the alleyway, your senses will heighten. You will feel the wind blowing against your skin. Your senses are so heightened you could hear even a pin drop. This is your brain upregulating what the nerves are saying and making them more sensitive. A month earlier, before the mugging, as you walked through the alleyway and the wind breezed against your skin, nerves in your skin and your brain would have had a little conversation.

Nerves- "Hey something touching us"

Brain- "Yeah don't worry about that"

Nerves – "Seriously brain, you might want to check this out"

Brain- "Honestly nerves, don't worry about it, we walk through here all the time. The book of life says we haven't had any problems here and based on all of the information coming in from other sources, I'm pretty happy to just create a light touch sensation where the wind is hitting the skin."

Nerves- "Ok then brain, you're the boss, we will shut up.

Your amazing brain can override and dampen how noisy your nerves are! But, it also has the ability to amplify them. Let's jump forward to one week after the mugging and you are now walking through the alleyway again. The wind blows against your skin, nerves in your skin and your brain will talk again, but this time it's different.

Nerves- "Hey brain, something is touching us"

Brain- "Yeah don't worry...oh.... hold on a second, - ok the book of life says the last time we were here we got mugged!"

Brain- "Ok, I want a lot more information from you down there, slightest change, doesn't matter what it is, I want to know, so start shouting"

Nerves "Ok boss, we will just keep shouting information up"

Remember, the Subconscious You who controls everything autonomic, also tells your nerves how sensitive they can be. It's safe to say that after being mugged, Subconscious You will tell the nerves to heighten and become more sensitive the next time you encounter that alleyway. Creating that particular output kept you safe, meaning it's going to get marked down as working and

Subconscious You will reinforce that behaviour. However, depending on the individual, you may become sensitive every time you walk down any alleyway, perhaps even during the day. Remember, Subconscious You has only one job and that's to keep you safe. If a little bioplasticity in the form of making nerves more sensitive or producing feelings of anxiety faster stops your from going down the alley and thus keeps you safe, then that's a job well done. Because pain is an output and also a pretty good tool to stop you doing something that Subconscious You doesn't want you to do, then because of bioplasticity, pain can begin to be used all the time. This means that instead of sitting in the cinema and getting a little bit stiff after an hour, your brain kicks outs pain instead!

Research Evidence for Bioplasticity

Mairi: I read Adam's words and they made perfect sense to me. I can relate to the experiences he has described and I can see how they would relate to the pain I experienced. I even remember studying bioplasticity as a psychology undergraduate. However, when I looked for academic papers about bioplasticity I found precisely none! I searched all of the usual academic databases for any information about the topic with no results found. I scoured the academic textbooks in the university library (turns out there is a library in the university! Who knew?!) Hell, I even committed the academic crime of googling it. Bioplasticity is not yet an academic thing. How can this be? There is one academic who has mentioned it in an internet post; Professor Lorimer Moseley from the

University of South Australia, a world leader in neuroscience and physiotherapy, all round clever cookie bun and Adam's "Man crush". I would definitely urge you to check out the web site for his research group www.bodyinmind.org. It is readable, understandable and entertaining, something that is rare in cutting edge academic research.

Professor Moseley first wrote about bioplasticity in 2014 when he declared himself to be, until then, a neurocentric: someone who focussed mainly on the impact of the brain on the body's functions. He admitted that, as a highly respected and experienced pain clinician and researcher, he had focussed on pain and how it is processed in the brain. Neuroplasticity is something that has a significant research history and has been explored at length in academic papers (and is the thing I thought I had learned about as a psychology student). Neuroplasticity is what happens when the way our brains function changes over the course of our lives. In other words, how our brains work isn't hard-wired. It can change to fit our needs, usually by training or to compensate for injury.

Training the brain to improve mental performance is not a new concept, but it isn't without its controversy. There is a famous experiment which involved a group of London taxi drivers (Maguire et al, 2000). In the days before satellite navigation, a London taxi driver had to learn every route in London, memorising a huge amount of information before they could be granted a cab licence. This process was called "Doing the Knowledge" and often took two or three years to complete. One of the key areas of the brain used for this type of memory feat is called the hippocampus, a small, seahorse shaped region in the medial temporal lobe of the brain. The brains of taxi drivers who had completed The Knowledge were scanned using Magnetic Resonance Imaging and the hippocampus areas were compared to non-taxi drivers of around the same age. The hippocampi of the taxi drivers were significantly larger in all cases! The area of the brain that stores encyclopaedic information actually grew bigger to accommodate the extra information these guys had to store to let them do their job. Now, a word of caution must be mentioned here. Unfortunately, the scientist in me reminds me that we cannot determine causation from correlation. Just because the people who had passed The Knowledge had larger hippocampi, we cannot tell if this is a cause or effect connection. It may be that people with larger hippocampi chose this profession because they had good memories, or only people with a larger hippocampus could pass the compulsory test. The researchers tested this by taking measurements before the training took place and it turns out, yes, the hippocampus did grow in size as The Knowledge was acquired!

In recent years, there have been many attempts to test the claims that manufacturers use to sell "brain training" games (Owen et al., 2010, for example). The companies claim that by working on different types of puzzles, skills like memory, vocabulary and arithmetic can be increased. This is an attractive idea, that we can build up abilities in certain brain functions by practising these puzzle-solving activities but at the time of writing, the evidence of their effectiveness beyond the actual games isn't there. Yes, people can improve their ability to finish crosswords or solve Sudoku problems, but the skills involved are restricted to just those areas. Playing the games does not improve language or number skills more generally. The studies are just beginning to emerge, though, and there is hope that improvements in the training and more stringent scientific testing will make the investigations more effective. We'll just have to wait and see if this research area gives us more information on precisely how and to what extent specific brain functions can be trained.

I've read about how the brain can change how it works after injury to compensate for damaged areas. If the part of the brain that deals with speech is injured, for example, other areas can take up the functions that are needed to talk. The brain effectively rewires itself, allowing the person to recover some ability that had been lost due to illness or injury. The most complex organ in our body can adjust to potentially catastrophic changes to support what people need to survive. We're only just beginning to understand how this happens and what we can do to help the rewiring on its way, but the possibilities for recovering lost brain function are a very exciting future development which could improve the quality of life for so many people.

So, if this ultra-complex part of our body can change its functioning to respond to our changing needs, can some of our simpler body structures do the same? Of course they can! They do it all the time. Take the heart for example. Did you know it can grow or shrink depending on what is happening to it? (Hill & Olson, 2008). During pregnancy, for example, the size of a woman's heart increases by 12%. The growing baby needs to have nutrients and oxygen delivered and waste products siphoned off and to do this, the mother's heart needs to pump more blood around her body. To handle this, the heart grows bigger, normally returning to the pre-pregnancy size within three months of delivery. In contrast, not moving can cause the heart to decrease by between 15-25% in overall size! Again, normal size can be regained once movement begins again. So, an input (greater or lesser demand on heart function) causes the physical structure of the heart to be altered (the output).

Our brains and our bodies can change how they function, based on what we do and what we expect to be able to do. We adapt to the circumstances we find ourselves in and settle into a stable pattern of responses, a situation that's called homeostasis. So, what does this mean for people who suffer with chronic pain? It turns out that our brains and our bodies can learn to be in pain and make that our default condition. Our homeostasis as chronic pain suffers is a state where we are in constant pain, functioning from this as our baseline position. Bioplasticity can help by giving us a way to change our homeostasis position. We need to find a way to stop this happening and set a new pain-free normal for our experience of life. This will happen if we just get moving, keep moving and move properly.

Part Two

Getting Ready to Get Better

What We Know So Far

Mairi: There's been a lot to take in from what you've read up to now so perhaps this would be a good time to take stock of what we've learned so far. Before you began suffering with this chronic pain, it's likely that something happened. An accident, an illness or an upsetting event. Usually with fibromyalgia there's something that triggers the whole experience. You will normally have some sort of recovery time following this trigger event. You may have had bone or tissue damage, or a medical operation to treat the condition. You may have had healing time after a bacterial or viral infection. You may have had some therapy or medication for mental health issues. Either way, there would be a time when your doctors, hopefully, supported active healing in the hope that the initial cause of your pain would get better.

Then you would have noticed the early symptoms of fibromyalgia. You would have begun to notice pain and stiffness in the morning, which may or may not have become easier as the day went on. The pain would have been not only in the area where any injury or illness had affected, but would have been in a number of areas throughout your body. The pain could have taken many forms. It may have been burning or crushing, aching or sharp, but it would be almost every day and would not get better over time.

You might have had good days and bad days. Some days the pain would appear to be less intense and, on those days, you are likely to have been able to be fairly active. Unfortunately, you may have taken that opportunity to catch up on things that had previously slipped. You won't have been as active on the days when the pain was worse so you might have thrown yourself into work, housework, gardening or leisure on the days when you were feeling better. As a result, you end up in a "flare up" situation, where the pain is much worse and may even leave you immobilised.

Flare ups could occur at any time in any place. You may wake up some days in extreme pain, much worse than what you usually experience. It can happen after a period of exertion or after a stressful experience. You may even be able to feel the pain increasing as a flare up begins. You might experience a flare up if you get too cold, or if you get too warm, or if you're in a particularly noisy or busy place. Some foods might trigger a flare up, or being in a dusty space, or in an uncomfortable seat. Or for actually no reason whatsoever, you might find that for a period of days or weeks, your pain has intensified and all you could do was to wait for it to go back to its normal levels and give you some sort of respite.

Along with the pain, you will have felt terrible crushing exhaustion. You will have found more and more that you are shattered during the day, unable to keep your eyes open, yet probably not sleeping well at night time. Perhaps you had trouble getting to sleep, or the pain would keep you awake, or you would wake for some other reason frequently through the night. When it's time to get up in the morning, you were unrefreshed, still very tired, yet you had another day to face of this crushing experience.

You have suffered, for a significant period of time, perhaps many years. Your pain and other symptoms were not imagined, not exaggerated and definitely not made up. You have done your best to cope with a horrible situation which has only become worse over time. Your medical team have told you there is no cure for fibromyalgia and the treatments they have offered have had little or no impact on your suffering. So why now, after all of this, are you able to turn this around and actually become well again?

Remember Adam's really bad joke about the chicken crossing the road earlier in the book? He told the story of his understanding of what the joke means. As a child, he took a literal meaning because he didn't have much of an understanding of life, death and suicidal chickens. As an adult, he was able to make a different sense out of the story because he had gathered information and understanding about more areas of life. New knowledge and a different perspective gave what he knew already new meaning. It's exactly the same for you as you begin to recover from fibromyalgia. The best brains you know have told you that you're stuck with this horrible situation and all of these symptoms. Your own research will have backed this up. Perhaps people you know and trust who have also been diagnosed will say the same thing. So how can it be that some people have already recovered from this painful experience?

It's all to do with finding out more about pain and understanding it from the new position that's emerging from leading researchers across the world. The traditional view of pain and what it's for has been built from understanding what's known as acute pain. Acute pain is what you experience after illness, injury or stress that affects you for a period of time, reduces gradually or quickly and then eventually goes away. That's what doctors have typically dealt with in the past and that's what they like to deal with now. Something that they can diagnose, treat and cure with a clean and positive ending so their patients can be discharged and go on to lead normal pain-free lives. What happens with fibromyalgia, however, is that the patterns of modern day life have got in the way and helped the pain to become a chronic experience. Perhaps we haven't taken the time to recover that we should have, or we haven't had the support from others that might have been offered in previous generations. We have had an expectation of "cure" that may or may not have come true. We have returned to jobs or to a daily life which was not helpful for someone with a high degree of pain. Perhaps you have been sitting at a desk or in a car, bus or train for extended periods, walking in shoes which are not designed for comfort, carrying heavy bags over one shoulder or stooping to look at a screen for long period of time. Any of our daily activities has the potential to cause pain and stiffness and, when you're already aware of pain in your body, this adds to the experience and makes the pain signals more intense.

The one thing I could predict about my fibromyalgia was that it would be unpredictable. Like an errant husband, I could always rely on it to be totally unreliable. If I felt a bit better one day, I would try to catch up with things I had previously wanted to do and this usually started a kind of boom and bust cycle. If I had a bit of relief from the pain I would throw myself into a flurry of activity. Inevitably this would bring on a crash and I'd end up suffering more because of it. I think I had come to recognise some things that would almost certainly cause a flare up: high stress, physical overactivity, extremes of hot or cold for example. But often, the flare ups seemed to come out of the blue and I was never sure of what, if anything, the trigger might be. I wondered if it might be something I had eaten and I kept a food diary for a while to see if there was anything I was sensitive to. I considered environmental toxins, changed to organic and natural cleaning products, thinking perhaps the flare ups might be a reaction to a particular chemical. I even made a weather chart and mapped it against my symptoms in case too much humidity/pollen/air pressure/bright sunshine (rarely a problem in Scotland!) was to blame. Unfortunately, none of these ideas helped me find out what caused the changes in my condition and confirmed to me the random nature of the beast. This was one of the most upsetting things about fibromyalgia. It seemed to me that, if I managed to plan and prepare to do something that I really wanted to do, this cruel monster of fibro would wait until the last minute before flashing the red card of flare up and all my hopes for a bit of fun would crash and burn. Of course, this was upsetting for me and almost certainly compounded the misery of having this horrible experience, but for other people it was equally frustrating. Friends and family would offer to do things with me and look forward to these themselves, only to find that I would cancel on them at the very last minute. This would happen repeatedly and eventually, people get fed up of the cycle and the invitations dried up. It's one of the main reasons why having a chronic condition leaves the sufferer isolated and lonely, separate from the rest of the world and with very poor quality of life.

Your Story of Recovery

Your path to recovery is likely to be full of surprises and for a while, you are likely to be in a place where the only constant thing will be change. As human beings, we don't like change and uncertainty. It causes us stress which makes a great deal of sense. If we don't understand what is going on and what is going to happen next, how do we know that we are in a safe place? Recovering from fibromyalgia will test you in ways you cannot possibly predict, so to keep your thoughts under control, I would like to suggest that you write out what's happening as if you were writing your own book or film about your life story. Choose the way that you think would be most fun and easiest for you to do. You can write in a Word document or blog (it doesn't have to be published but it can be if you want that to happen). You can set up a social media account where you can dump your thoughts – again it's up to you whether you keep it private or public. Or (shock horror) what about a physical piece of paper or notebook? Start at the beginning. Look at Adam and my stories at the start of the book. Where did your pain story start? When did you first notice the symptoms? What did it feel like? How did it affect you? Are there are pictures or images that sum up what was going on? Is there a colour for your pain? Is it red, gooey green, black, hot white? What pattern does it make? Is it zigzag, spikey, rolling up and down, or a straight line maybe?

You might want to include a brief section on what's changed in your life since you became aware of the chronic pain. Now this is where I will issue a warning. There is likely to be a pretty sad list of things that may have happened to you. This is not a time to be dwelling in a "poor me" state. Quite the opposite. The idea is to recognise the things that have happened and make a note of them, not to become stuck in a wallowing exercise. Try to see the positive in your list. The fact that you've survived through all of it and you're strong enough emotionally to start to turn things around makes you remarkable. So remarkable, in fact, that I want you to imagine that Hollywood have snapped up the film rights to your life story. You are going to be a classic "triumph over tragedy" (side note: if this does happen please do invite Adam and me to the premiere. We love a good night at the movies). Who would play you in this inspirational story? Which actor do you think would be able to do the story justice? Add a picture of them to your writing. Keep in mind you will have to be involved in their direction and in writing the script which lets them play the part of you.

The next part of your story is the key scene. It's the part of the movie where the lead actor turns their world around. This is where you are right now. It happens because you now know things you didn't know before. Write down what you've learned so far and why this will give you a chance to make the change. You know that there are myths around pain and that it doesn't necessarily mean that you are damaging or injuring yourself when you feel pain. You know that chronic pain is different from acute pain which is being felt to protect you. When pain becomes chronic it may have become your new normal – your everyday experience and base line for living. It is not serving a purpose for you, but your brain has become used to making pain, so continues to do so as your default position. You know that there are ways to re-educate your brain and ease it back into a normal non-pain state. Later, you will read about the movements you can make that will help this to happen safely and effectively. You know that pain is not a natural state and you have learned about how your brain has produced the output of pain in your life. Be sure you understand this before going any further. Pain is an output and your brain is designed to produce that output. You are now learning how to stop this happening so “no pain” becomes your new normal state.

Support groups

Barriers to Recovery

Adam: People recover from fibro every day. You just don't see it. In the past, some people who had recovered have tried to write about it in online support groups, only to be met with aggression and/or hatred. For a place that is meant to offer support to those who are chronically ill, online support groups are the last place you will find support for recovery and indeed they can be a very dangerous place. Well-wishers are told "Well then you didn't really have fibro" or "Well your fibro wasn't as bad as mine" or any other saying that removes them from being accountable for their actions or adds justification as to why someone might be able recover, but they themselves cannot. In these groups you will find people playing with their illness, in the way that children play "top trumps", constantly trying to outdo each other in terms of illness and disability. Unfortunately, any post that may hint of the possibility of recovery, a news article that hints at positivity or a post by someone who is writing about having a good three-week run is often ignored or deleted. However, any post about the plight of one's suffering or "I wish there was a cure" can receive likes and comments in the hundreds and can quickly drown out any positive posts.

It's also important not to forget the dangerous information that can be shared in these groups. Factually inaccurate information can be found by the boat load in online support groups. This information can vary, but you don't have to look very far to find a post that spouts some nonsense. Among other things, such nonsense includes;

- The bodies of people with fibro need to work eight times harder to function than those of a "healthy person"
- There is no research being done on fibromyalgia
- Fibromyalgia is a disease, and no one believes that it's real.

It's important to remember that such claims are indeed, complete nonsense! There is no evidence to suggest that the first claim is even remotely true. For the second point, from 2012-2017 there were over 9000 research papers published on fibromyalgia, which shows without a doubt that research is being done. However, with that being said, the experts still don't agree on causes and treatments any more than they did twenty years ago. This also supports the argument that fibro is not a cause and effect disease, merely a word. In fact, speaking from personal opinion and years of experience here, a large percentage of those diagnosed with fibromyalgia are actually hypermobile and because of the associated tissue laxity, symptoms can present as very systemic.

Online support groups over the years have turned Fibromyalgia Syndrome (remember this means collection of symptoms) into a culturally adopted disease, turning it into something it's definitely not. Fibromyalgia is a word used to describe the condition of somebody who has a collection of symptoms for which the medical world can find no pathological cause. Those with this label are indeed in pain and yes, it can be absolutely debilitating. However, fibromyalgia is not a disease, it is label which is given when numerous medical professionals do not have a good enough understanding of the Biopsychosocial influences on pain. This is evident by the fact that they still freely offer out nerve blocks and cortisone injections, working from the outdated Cartesian Model of Pain from the 1600s. The Cartesian Model of Pain created by Rene Descartes thought of pain as a stimulus created by the tissues which would send pain messages to the brain. Obviously, it is now outdated and known to be highly inaccurate as we know pain can exist without the presence of tissue damage.

All in all, many people do recover, but after they attempt to help others and are shot down, they simply just get on with their lives and most people don't even realise they have left the support group. This is our next step on our journey: leaving the online and physical support groups. Remember, people do not like it when others recover, as it causes a state of psychological stress called cognitive dissonance as new information conflicts with their existing beliefs. Recovery needs to be your everything from now on: you need to eat it, sleep it and be it. Negative experiences in support groups have no benefit towards your recovery and in fact hinder recovery with unhelpful comments, misinformation and the worst of all, acceptance of the situation.

Evidence For and Against

Mairi: Whew strong words! I've been a member of online support groups for fibromyalgia for years now and I have certainly seen the kind of thing Adam describes. But, as a scientist, I have to consult published peer-reviewed academic research to find out what the impartial view is on their usefulness.

A group of scientists based in Toronto, Canada published a systematic literature review in the British Medical Journal in 2005 looking at exactly this topic. A systematic literature review searches all the important sources of academic research to identify everything that's been studied about a particular topic, in this case fibromyalgia and online support groups. They search these papers identifying those which meet really tough scientific criteria for the way they were carried out. The papers that pass this scrutiny are then examined in detail and a consensus view is achieved. When the paper was published in 2005 no studies of the impact of fibromyalgia support groups met the quality criteria for inclusion in the review. Doh! Unfortunately, at the time of writing, no systematic review has been published looking at the impact of support groups on people diagnosed with Fibromyalgia Syndrome.

The next step that an academic will take to get information about a topic is to look at the individual published papers in the area. A study which looked at Dutch online support groups interviewed frequent posters to identify what benefits they got from the group (van uden-Kraan et al., 2008). The participants in the study said that taking part in the groups made them feel empowered, helped them feel emotionally supported and understood. People who volunteered their views mainly saw the experience as positive and empowering. However, the researchers point out that these views may not be representative of everyone who uses online support groups. The people who took part were highly active posters on the sites. People who tend to read more than they post and people who left the group, perhaps because they were dissatisfied, were not represented in the research. However, it's appropriate to point out that the researchers found that for some people, being an active part of an online support group was viewed as a positive experience.

Other researchers have reported some of the negative aspects of online support groups. A Nottingham-based group found that more than half of the people they surveyed who had used an online support group for infertility talked about the disadvantages (Malik & Coulson, 2010). These included reading about ongoing negative experiences, being exposed to inaccurate information and a feeling of being "drawn in", that being part of the group was becoming an almost addictive experience. If you're just starting your journey into wellness, you'll know that it can be difficult, frustrating and even painful sometimes. The last thing you will need is exposure to anything but positive encouragement, so I would really urge you to stop reading posts from groups that might discourage your efforts.

Fibromyalgia can be a very isolating experience. We will all have felt that people don't understand the level of suffering we endure with it and it's not uncommon for sufferers to feel that they aren't believed. It can look like there's nothing wrong so the general public can often be unsympathetic to people who are in chronic pain. An interesting paper published in 2008 gave a good report of what people who have been diagnosed with fibromyalgia feel about their condition (van Wilgen, van Ittersum, Kaptein & van Wijhe, 2008). The researchers found that people with fibromyalgia did not expect the treatments they were likely to be offered would be of much help and that their condition would be long lasting and problematic. Levels of personal control of the condition were lower than people who had other conditions such as rheumatoid arthritis, for example. It's not surprising, then, that finding some solace and understanding from other sufferers helps people to feel less isolated with the condition. However, the researchers also go on to say that focussing on the negative aspects of the condition and expecting things to remain the same or get worse is actually likely to make the symptoms worse. This is why you need to be really careful about what information you are exposed to when you begin your journey towards wellness.

It is possible to break free of chronic pain and recover from this horrible condition. But it will be difficult and you will have setbacks along the way. You will need to be determined and resourceful and keep going despite the barriers you will come across. Support from loved ones will make a positive difference but might not always be available. You will need to call on all of your reserves to make the changes you need to make to recover and you'll also need to make some difficult decisions on what you have to let go. Online support groups may have been your only source of comfort, maybe for quite some time. You will have made friends and shared information that perhaps nobody else knows about. Keep in touch with people who are supportive and open to the very real possibility of recovery. Sadly, you might need to cut off ties from people who don't support you or who firmly believe there is no cure. When you're better and living life to the full, you can reconnect and move forward, but during your process of recovery, it might be necessary to take a step back. Perhaps your journey to wellness will change their minds in future but for now, you have to prioritise yourself and look after number one. Get well. Then you'll have the chance to be positive and supportive to others as they take their first steps to being pain free.

Please be in absolutely no doubt:

- We believe that you are suffering pain.
- We believe that your pain is real.
- We believe it's not just your imagination.
- We believe you're not exaggerating.
- We believe you're not looking for sympathy or attention.
- We believe that you are not weak.
- We believe that you have not caused this by choices you have made.
- We believe you have tried lots of things in the past that you thought might help.
- We believe that you are fed up watching life pass you by.
- We believe you want to stop taking unnecessary medications and suffering the side effects from these.

We also believe that you want to get better. Why else would you read this book?

We have both experienced negative judgements from other people about our pain. As Adam said from the start, you can't think it away or just will yourself to ignore it. You need to understand it in order to overcome it. This book will help you do just that. No matter how long pain has been a part of your everyday life, it's never too late to change. You only get one life. Yes, you've had years where your enjoyment of life has been affected by this horrible pain. Make that a part of your history, and get yourself ready now to move into a new pain-free chapter of your life.

Why is this Treatment Not Available on the NHS?

Mairi: This is a really good question and one that is mainly due to the process of scientific research. It wasn't until I studied for my first psychology degree that I really understood how science works. Every new idea that revolutionises what we know about the world is not really new at all! It comes from ideas that have previously existed, sometimes in different forms, that get put together in new ways to come up with exciting developments. It's all based on the idea that we are Standing on the Shoulders of Giants, as Sir Isaac Newton said in the seventeenth century. Sure, researchers and scientists will sometimes have an "aha" moment when a new idea occurs to them, but to make it real, they have to prove it based on what we already know. Serendipity, when something potentially positive happens by chance may be life changing in Hollywood movies but to a scientist, it's useless unless it's based on previously known facts. That's the unromantic truth about the world of research! This principle works across the board whether you're proposing a new treatment for fibromyalgia, exploring particle physics or looking for a way to grow drought resistant crops in arid climates. New ideas have to be based on what we already know.

So, what happens when someone comes up with a radical new way of thinking that could improve the lives of millions at no cost and regardless of age, gender or background? Surely there would be an exception and it would be taken up straight away, especially if there are no side effects from drugs or danger to life? Sadly, no. That's not how it works. Even if somebody stumbles across a new cure for the worst cancers in the world, it won't become a thing until it's been through the proper processes.

Adam wasn't prepared to put up with a lifetime of pain and misery and he went about reading and finding out everything he could about recovering from chronic pain to help himself get better. Some of the sources of information would be dubious and many would come from the place of "well I tried it and it worked". He tried a lot of things and finally found what worked, for him and for countless others. And the rest is history. I tried the same approach and that's how I found Adam. He didn't advertise himself, I had to find him. He keeps his practice growing purely by word of mouth and his list of previous clients who have gone on to lead happy pain free lives continues to grow, because he read and considered and tried what made sense.

For years before finding Adam, I did the same thing. I tried everything I could afford and some things did make a difference for a while, or improved things slightly, helping to lift my spirits and keep going. Nothing made the huge and lasting improvement that Adam's approach did, which is why this book has been written. It's a grass roots way to try to spread the word about something that works and that you can try yourself, bypassing the years of work it takes to get the approach taken up widely, so that eventually everyone can benefit from the method as the first line of treatment for chronic pain.

Having said all this, NHS consultants do refer people to Adam for treatment. He has been approached by many professionals from rheumatology, general practice and psychology who have reviewed what he does and recommended it personally to their patients. He doesn't seek to set up a formal referral process, however, because part of taking his approach is making your own decision to get better, and putting up with the hard work it takes to do so. Getting moving again is painful in the beginning and it's extremely difficult to keep motivated and push on. To do so, you need to be absolutely committed to getting better and if you're following a referral process, there's a chance that you just see it as part of the same old treadmill of things that don't work or take too much effort. To really succeed, you need to find the solution, want it to work and be prepared to give everything you can to get better. If you've read this far in the book, you've got the first one in the bag. By the end of the book, you should have all three of these goals covered.

So, I hear you ask, why has nobody else come up with this wonderful way to cure chronic pain? Surely the leading researchers of the world have access to the same information. Why aren't they testing the same process that Adam uses? Well, some are, and I'll talk a bit about that in a moment. But for now, let's suppose that a pain scientist decides he wants to take a radical approach, scours the internet, finds the Fibro Guy and thinks Eureka, I'm going to test this method, claim it as my own and get a Nobel prize for medicine. They can only do this by referencing previously published research which supports their new idea. So first they need to introduce the radical concept that pain is not necessarily an indicator of damage. That's in progress but it's a seismic shift in thinking that will only be fully accepted once hundreds of researchers have tested every possible scenario in every possible type of patient and they have published their findings that support this.

Assuming that has happened, we now have a theory of pain which can be used to show why pain happens when there is no source of damage. Then, hundreds more researchers, because typically theoretical scientists aren't the same group of people as those who test interventions, need to read the findings and be prepared to change their existing protocols that have been built up over many years to take into account the new thinking. Each individual aspect of each therapy needs to be adjusted to consider the new principles of pain. Only one variable can be changed at a time, for this is the scientific method, to be absolutely sure that the new approach which is being tested is the one which is making a positive difference. Again, each change needs to be tested in every type of patient in every scenario to make sure it is globally effective before a link can be established between this new development and improvements in people's health. Of course, there will be scientists who don't agree and they will carry out counter research which aims to challenge the new thinking by showing it isn't effective in getting rid of pain. These challenges will be helpful because they will make the researchers who are testing the new approach consider aspects that they maybe hadn't thought of, or they will highlight uncertainty and encourage more research into the areas where perhaps recovery isn't as obvious or immediate. But, as you would imagine, this will take a while.

So once a link between the new approach to pain and getting better has been established, does this mean that the therapy can be rolled out now? Of course not. Just because there is a link between the two it doesn't mean that one makes the other happen. The researchers now need to prove that the treatment is effective by carrying out randomised controlled trials and by monitoring the results over many years. They need to be sure that the treatment causes the cure, that it's not influenced by other factors, that it works as well as or better than existing treatments and that the results are permanent. Once all of this is done, a structured literature review will take place and guidelines for treatment can finally be recommended and adopted. But that's not all going to happen overnight.

I was an academic myself for many years, although not in the field of pain research. It's a sad truth that funding for research is becoming ever more competitive and the big money goes to the big names who are well established and working in a "sexy" area. New ideas from early career researchers have no chance of getting off the ground unless they are adopted by one of the big guns. Often, the early career researchers are challenging ideas that people have built highly successful academic profiles on so you can probably see that this isn't easy to achieve. But it does happen. Professor Moseley at the University of South Australia is one. So are his colleagues at Brunel University, John Hopkins University, University of Milano-Bicocca, University College London, University of Washington, Greifswald, Cape Town, Kings College London, Oxford University, the list goes on and on. These scientists and others are making great progress in changing how we think about and treat chronic pain, but before this gets adopted into mainstream practice, a whole lot of work needs to be done.

This work is generally funded by large global organisations who offer funds which rival groups of researchers compete to win. These are often councils funded by contributions from government (which comes originally from taxpayers) or large charitable organisations. A significant portion of research is funded by pharmaceutical companies. Remember, the people who suffer from chronic pain typically take substantial quantities of drugs for the rest of their life. Research to support Adam's methods would ultimately reduce the number of drugs which are sold worldwide. I'll just leave that thought with you for now. It is important to understand that this lengthy testing process happens for a reason. Before a licensed health professional can recommend a treatment, they have to be sure that it is effective and most importantly, that it will do no harm. This type of stringent testing is essential to avoid the catastrophes that have happened in the past due to unforeseen bad drug treatment outcomes and this must be avoided at all costs. But progress is being made and I'm sure in due course, you will read about the outstanding developments that are being made in pain research.

For now, we have a solution that you might just find works for you, as it has for me and countless others. Until the researchers have a chance to jump through the hoops they need to in order to provide recommendations to the medical profession, you might like to consider trying the process for yourself. If you do and you are committed to it, you can start getting better now, today, and save yourself years of misery by doing so.

A Word About Procrastination

Pro¦cras¦tin¦a¦tion¦

(Noun)

The action of delaying or postponing action.

Examples:

"My advice is, never do tomorrow what you can do today. Procrastination is the thief of time. Collar him! (Charles Dickens)

"Life is what happens to you when you're busy making other plans" (John Lennon)

"Procrastinate now! Don't put it off" (Ellen DeGenres).

You might say that I'm a born procrastinator but I say just you wait and see! (Mairi Harper).

Getting Things Done

Mairi: Having written 100,000 words of a PhD thesis, I could claim to be a person who gets things done. However, I did receive excellent guidance, encouragement and cajoling from a couple of superb PhD supervisors who I didn't dare disappoint! As far as pretty much everything else goes, I'm not really a self-starter it's true to say. Attention span of a goldfish is a better description, like the fish Dory from the film Finding Nemo. (Cue a quick exploration of the internet to find out what species of fish Dory was meant to be). When something needs to be done that I really don't want to do right now, I suddenly develop a deep interest in how factories manufacture cinnamon buns and, as if by magic, there's a programme on TV that can show me the answer right now. I'll just need to sit for the next thirty minutes and then this knowledge will be revealed. And after that, I'll get straight onto the job that needs done. After I clear out that kitchen drawer because I'll need the heart rate monitor to check my pulse rate. That's important, right? And I can't go out and do things without a decent jacket, it's cold outside. So, I need to find that super warm fleece which I put away somewhere to keep safe. Ooh, squirrel!

You get the picture. It's amazing how long it can take a person to just get started on something that holds very little appeal to them, even though they know it's what they really should do and bizarrely enough, even when they know it will make them better. This was definitely the case for me with Adam's online videos. I watched them through once, because it's good practice to see what's involved from start to finish. I also wanted to check that I had everything I would need close by and that I had enough space to carry out the movements he was showing me. Even though the sessions were short, by the time I'd watched them I could easily find something that required my immediate attention and would wander off to attend to this. I would get back to the videos immediately afterwards, I promised myself, as soon as I had just done this important task that had to be done right now.

Sigh. Even when I knew that these sessions would make the world of difference to my life and would reduce the pain I was feeling, I still put them off. It's like there's a big red self-destruct button labelled "I'm not worthy" that I just feel the need to press, especially when I've got something that will actually make life better for me. I wonder if you feel the same way sometimes? Putting yourself and your own needs pretty far down the list of priorities? Kids, partners, parents, pets, friends, family, neighbours, homeless dogs – anything and anyone deserves your energy more than yourself? This is not true. Persuading you to feel better about yourself and to increase your own self-esteem is a whole other book, so I'm not going to go into this in too much detail now, but I will share my own tip for helping to prioritise doing what you need to do to feel better. Remember the advice from airline cabin crew saying, "fit your own oxygen mask before helping others"? If you prioritise yourself and your health, you absolutely will be in a better place to help others. You'll be stronger and have more to give so ultimately the others that you want to help will be better off. If you can't bring yourself to believe that your health is worth enough to invest your time in, do it to improve your ability to help others. Any way you want to look at it is fine, just make sure you make time (as a priority) to move and keep moving to improve your health and stay well. You know it makes sense.

Making a Start

Having read this far in the book, you'll know by now why you are experiencing chronic pain and you will also know that there is something you can do to get better. You will also know that this will only happen if you make it so. The best way to make sure that you do the work that needs done is to get ready to sort out the barriers that you think might stop you from moving towards wellness. Try to anticipate and solve any problems that might pop up before they stop you in your tracks. This is a good thing to write down and pin up somewhere where you can see it. For me, finding the time was a key concern. I had hoped to set aside thirty minutes a day to follow the programme that Adam had set me. If your own plans involve a different approach to movement by swimming, walking, gym class or whatever, you might be planning a similar time to devote to the tasks. So, when would this event take place? It couldn't be first thing in the morning because I would be getting the kids ready for school. As the day went on, in the beginning I was still feeling a bit rough so thought it would be better to wait till the pain had eased off a bit before starting. As lunchtime approached I was beginning to get tired so I thought I'd be better to have lunch first, hope that I got a bit more energy from that and then I would start my programme for the day. After lunch, I crashed out through fatigue, waking in time to collect the kids from school. Then it would be a case of finding out what had happened in their day and supervising homework before getting dinner ready. By the evening I would be exhausted and doing any movement would just not be an option. So where do I fit in the thirty minutes of planned activity?

Looking back through this description, I can see that I was prioritising my limited energy reserves towards my kids. As a mum, they were my top priority and I had enough guilt about how little I could do with them that I owed it to them to give them the basics. The only way I could find the time to do what needed to be done was to make myself think about the outcome I wanted above everything else at that time: to be able to be a better, stronger, more active mum for them. It came down to the simplest truth. If I kept doing what I had been doing until then, they would still have the mum who could do hardly anything with them. If I made the commitment to follow the programme I hoped would improve my health, they might have a mum who could do so much more with and for them. It was a no brainer.

To make sure I made time for the movement I hoped would make me better, I decided to do it every day at 8am. I set an alarm on my phone and no matter what I was doing, how I was feeling or how interesting the programme about debt collection was, I would get up and get going. That way I made sure I did the minimum every day without allowing anything else to get in the way.

However, a true procrastinator will not make things easy for themselves and they will always find other ways to stop themselves doing what they really need to do! A favourite of mine would be to regularly lose the bits and pieces I had looked out for the movements (timer, spikey rubber balls, even the massive inflatable Swiss ball for sitting on!). I want you to have a think about the type of things that might crop up for you. What might stand in your way of getting thirty minutes of movement every day? Make a list now and work out how to prevent these possible barriers from happening. Pin it up somewhere so you can see it and it won't get lost. Be ready to make your health a priority and it will repay you for the rest of your life. You won't regret it, for sure.

Worrying About Moving

The big worry, of course, is that moving more will cause a flare up of pain. The traditional medical advice is to pace yourself and not push yourself to far in order to avoid this. So how can you increase your daily movement and get fitter if you're not pushing for more movement? I'll let Adam deal with this question in a later chapter. Just be sure to do what is sensible and safe for you and you'll be fine.

One thing that will definitely help is if you have someone you can confide in and tell about your intention to move more. It's better if you can choose someone you know will be supportive and who wants you to get better, but this may not be the first person you would normally think of. It's a good idea to try the problem-solving approach you used for time thieves earlier when deciding who you will tell about your plans for getting better. Think about how improving your health will affect your relationship with that person. We hope that other people will be happy for us if we get better, but perhaps they feel that helping you gives them a sense of purpose or makes them feel they are doing something worthwhile. If you get better and don't need their support, this might affect the relationship they have with you. Consciously or subconsciously, they might therefore have doubts about whether they want to be 100% supportive of your efforts. Also, if this person has an illness themselves, especially if it includes chronic pain, how will you getting better make them feel? They may well be happy for you, but what do they think about their own health? Everybody reaches the point of making the decision to get better at different times in their lives. Your friend may not quite be ready to consider the path to wellness and your recovery challenges their view of themselves. They may think that their condition must be worse than yours was if you've managed to get better and this could affect what they believe about your understanding of their life. They could start to think that perhaps you weren't as ill as you said you were and they might begin to mistrust what you say about your health too. They probably don't know as much about chronic pain as you do now, having read this far in the book, so it may well be difficult for them to believe that it's possible to get better or that the results can last. All of these thoughts will affect how supportive they can be of your attempts to get better and, when you are well again, you'll be strong enough to deal with them. Hopefully, you'll also be compassionate enough to accept that your friend hasn't got to a place yet when they are able to consider taking control of their health. But whilst you're on the path to wellness, every ounce of emotional strength you have will be needed to keep you focus on getting better.

Having a chronic illness is usually associated with seeing a decline in your financial position. I definitely saw a huge drop in income and had no money whatsoever for gym membership or fancy equipment. But it's possible to make a start on your plan to move more without spending money you don't have. The third section of the book where Adam gets you started on moving will have activities you can do at no financial cost. The solution is available to everyone without having to spend money on pills, potions or pokey stuff. When you're on the mend, you might find that you're able to earn some money from paid employment, if you're not in that place now. Being disabled is expensive and it costs you to be ill! Getting better will reduce what you have to spend on things that help you get through life. Hopefully, you'll manage to get back some control and as time goes by, your condition will continue to improve. When you've recovered and got your health back, I would encourage you to pass on this book (if it's a hard copy) to a friend or charity shop. Spread the word as widely as possible that the solution to recovery from fibromyalgia is simple, cheap and available to everyone!

Footnote: if you're interested in the psychology behind getting to grips with procrastination and making the move towards fitness, I would recommend that you look at the Theory of Implementation Intention (IIS) (Gollwirzer, 1993). This theory considers the reasons why there is often a difference between what we intend to do and what we actually get done. There's been a massive amount of research in this field and it's truly fascinating, but I'm trying to stick to the knitting here and write specifically about relief from chronic pain!

Client Success Stories and Testimonials

Adam: I have had the privilege of working with some amazing people over the years, those who have worked hard with myself to create a better standard of living for themselves. Many clients, for various reason, like to stay anonymous after their programmes which is fine and perfectly understandable. However, others do not mind and hope their stories can be of inspiration to others.

You can read about some of my clients' journeys below.

Steph - Myalgic Encephalomyelitis

"I was recommended to Adam by a reflexologist I had visited and after looking at his blog and success stories, I felt this was the answer that I had been waiting years for.

I first fell ill seven years ago where I developed crippling fatigue, migraines, sore throats, brain fog and a lot of pain in my body overnight. At its worst, I had to crawl to move around the house as I didn't have enough energy to stand up. I would lie down to dry my hair and shower sitting on the bottom of the bath. I would generally be in bed by 7pm every night and one in every three weeks would sleep from 6pm on the Friday night after work, right through to the Monday morning as I was just so exhausted. I was even then falling asleep halfway through eating my tea a lot of the time. This continued flaring up over the years. I also had tight muscles through all of my body, which caused burning pain which made it difficult to sleep at times. On walking, I would get out of breath and was unable to get up more than one flight of stairs without having to rest to get my breath back and for the pain in my legs to calm down. At that point, although I was positive, there wasn't any signs that I would ever get better or any other treatment planned to resolve the issues I had. It seemed that I would be unable to ever have a social life again, do the things I enjoyed or do exercise. I was told I would have to work part time or not at all due to illness so when I finished a contract in a workplace, I then took this opportunity to take some time off to rest, really look after myself and get better, but even after six months the fatigue and other symptoms still persisted.

After the first week with Adam I could feel a difference and as I attended more sessions, my muscles stopped hurting, the burning sensation went and four weeks on I haven't had any episodes of fatigue, sore throats or headaches. I feel a lot stronger and like my body is working properly for the first time in years. As my body had been so exhausted, I had developed pompholyx eczema about five years ago, which meant most of the time I had difficulty using my hands and often enough not being able to use them at all for anything, including washing and eating. This has been healing over the time I have been seeing Adam. This is something that I had struggled with for years and tried everything and did not expect to happen. I am quite confident and positive that this will clear up completely in the coming few weeks. I'm so pleased that I went to see Adam and very happy with the work he has done and the support that he has given me to get my life back. It's great to feel like the old me again.

Five months after seeing Adam, I have no symptoms of the old problems. I no longer suffer fatigue, so can now have a social life. I have night times and weekends to do what I want and am happily making up for the time that I couldn't. I also have had no episodes of pompholyx eczema since, so can eat a meal without ever needing help. I don't need my husband to wash and dry my hair for me anymore, or ask my mum to come around to do it if he was working away. I have also lost three stone that the steroid drugs put on me for treatment of my hands during severe flare up. Adam completely changed by life for the better as I was to be honest in quite a lot of pain, a lot of the time, whether in my body or the pain and discomfort from my hands.

I also decided that I did not want to go back to work sitting in an office all day now that I can be so active, so I decided to set up my own business, working five to sometimes six days a week, around 38 hours a week doing a very physical job and still the old symptoms have not reappeared and I don't expect them to."

Carly - Hypermobile Ehlers-Danlos Syndrome

"I have just finished my 4th week with Adam. I'm 35, severely hypermobile (Beighton score 9/9) and was diagnosed with Ehlers-Danlos Syndrome Type 3, ten years ago. Since then I have suffered widespread chronic joint and muscle pain, particularly in my legs, back and neck. I also suffer chronic, almost daily migraines.

I was told by a series of doctors and specialists that I would be in pain for the rest of my life and that walking especially would always cause me terrible trouble. I've been through the usual meds as well as physio, osteopathy and Pilates - all of which made me feel worse, ramming home the message that I was using my body 'wrong' and had a 'weak core' and that the 'damage was already done'. This added to my physical tension, stiffness and pain. I forgot how to move naturally. For years I've been terrified to straighten my legs properly or relax my shoulders for fear of slouching or 'hanging off my joints'. I was so conscious of being upright I came to Adam basically walking like I had a stick up my backside! I felt that my body was weak and vulnerable, unstable and ready to fall apart at any time so I was carrying a ton of tension trying to hold it all together...

Adam's teachings have been a revelation to me. Working with him really is all about re-education and I have learned so much already. It's been very empowering for me to feel that I have it within me to take back control of my condition rather than handing myself over to so-called 'experts.' The difference between them and Adam is that they simply want you to do as they say because they 'know best'- whereas Adam talks to you 'on the level'- he has been there himself so he knows the pain and the struggle. He tells you literally everything about the process, making it accessible, easy to understand and often hilarious as well!!

The science behind his teachings is totally fascinating and 100% watertight. He is the first person I have approached for help who has been able to offer me something genuinely believable- and to explain in detail the workings behind it.

I have literally never met anyone as passionate and enthusiastic about what they do as Adam and his energy and enthusiasm are totally infectious! That's not to say I haven't hated him at times!! There have been moments in that gym where it has sounded like someone was actually giving birth (sorry about the swearing!) but it has been so worth it, and always ended up in lots of laughter. He has pushed me harder than I would ever have dared push myself, and helped me prove to myself that my body is strong and capable- not about to fall apart at any minute!!

After the first couple of weeks, I was able to give myself permission to slouch... to relax... to take the stick out of my backside and walk loosely and freely. Even that tiny change has had a big impact on how the whole of my body feels, getting rid of all that learned tension and fear. Adam has had me leaping about playing badminton, not worrying for a second that I was going to go over on my wobbly ankles or twist my knee.

After my third week I went on holiday for a fortnight and had the confidence to get rid of my special shoes and orthotics completely. I walked for miles every day in a pair of flip-flops and did not have so much as a single second of back, hip or knee pain of any kind- something I haven't experienced for years! I spent 17 hours on an aeroplane, cramped into a tiny seat, and hopped out at the end like nowt was the bother (meanwhile my non-hypermobile husband was groaning with pain and stiffness!)

At the end of week 3 I also had five solid days without the severe daily headache which has made my life hell for years. That is a HUGE step in the right direction. It's an ongoing process with the migraines, ups and downs, but I feel I'm gradually taking back control and when I have felt crap with it, Adam has been a great listener and helped me regain my focus and positivity again- 'Adam's Talking Therapies'

I can't recommend this program highly enough- if you come to it with an open mind, a willingness to learn, and a commitment to stick in and keep up with the training, I believe that it absolutely will give you the tools you need to start taking back your life. THANK YOU, ADAM, – looking forward to the next bit...!!"

Richard - Fibromyalgia

Richard came up to Newcastle for a workshop in January and he has been one of the best people to work with remotely. Richard has literally text every day and I'm really happy with how things are progressing!

“My name is Richard Lawrence (Age 66) and for the past two years, I have been suffering from Polymyalgia which was followed by Fibromyalgia which reverted back to Polymyalgia.

Two months ago, I got to the point where I had difficulty in climbing the stairs getting in and out of the car and many other normal everyday activities. This coupled with severe pain, which was soul destroying.

After blood tests which showed high ESR and CRP levels, a rheumatologist prescribed steroids (prednisolone) through my GP and stated that exercise is a good thing to help combat the condition. But due to the pain and discomfort, it was very difficult to get the motivation and push and drive to accomplish this without professional help.

I had tried several Physiotherapists to no avail. Trawling the internet I found Adam Foster (The Fibro Guy) and purchased the Fibromyalgia Graded Exercise Programme. I followed this with a 3-hour consultation with Adam in Newcastle which for me is a 400-mile round trip. This was invaluable. Following on from the consultation the personal exercise regime that Adam devised for me is incredible. All exercises hit the right areas but do become easier with time. He also backs this up with help and advice. I can honestly say that I have never felt so good and will continue with Adam’s programme.

I can see now how the physical can affect the psychological and that can affect the social as they all feed off one another, just like Adam taught me.

Good luck to Adam and long may he continue."

Stronger Than You Think

Muscles are not the Only Strong Ones

Adam: When every bone feels like lead, when every joint aches unrelentingly and the simplest of movements make you want to cry, then it's really easy to feel weak. Like we have mentioned before, the world around you hasn't changed, the inputs remain the same as when you last experienced them. However, the way they are processed is completely different now. Everything you do today will either reinforce a belief or it will start to break it down. The longer we are in pain, the weaker we feel and the weaker we feel, the weaker we become. If you only take one thing from this chapter, let it be this; muscles get too much attention! Ok, you may be wondering what I mean, that's understandable.

Muscle is tissue and it is ultimately controlled by the brain and nervous system. It is the brain that tells each muscle how strong it can be (within the amount of fibres it can recruit). It's the brain that tells a muscle how weak it can be and it's the brain that decides how much range of motion you can have with the muscle (how tight or flexible you are). When you don't have a brain, guess what happens to the muscles? Yes, you guessed it, absolutely nothing! Muscles and joints get all the attention, even fascia seems to be getting more attention now! You know, despite the fact it's mainly dead, is much too tough to "release" and correlates very poorly to chronic pain.

Strength Experiment

I tell you what, let's do a little home experiment, let's see how the brain controls the tissue. So, for this I would suggest you find someone to help.

1. Hold one arm out to the side, straight out from your shoulder.
2. Now get someone to put their hand on top of your hand.
3. Don't look at the other person; instead, focus on their hand, on your hand.
4. Ask the other person to pick a number between 1 and 10, but not to tell you.
5. Ask them to count to that number in their head and when they reach it, to try to push your arm down and when they do, I want you to resist.
6. Now you may have felt strong, you may have felt weak. However, based on the inputs your brain decided to recruit X amount of muscle fibres. Now, let's change the input slightly so that you can't recruit as many fibres. Let's make you instantly weaker! You are going to repeat the experiment again, but this time, as your partner starts counting in their head, I want you to close your eyes and resist when you feel them push down.

Feel how much weaker you are? Now remember, you haven't suddenly had a massive amount of muscle waste away nor has your partner suddenly got stronger. However, you did take a really important input away that we use for assessing potential danger:

Sight. You also slowed down a lot of postural reflexes, like transverse abdominal activation for example, which provide you with a lot of support for movement and strength. So, if we can create such a vast difference in strength by just altering the input, imagine what happens when we have been in pain for a long time and Subconscious You uses our past experiences in the book of life to protect us?

Age Related Concerns

I see this kind of output change a lot in my 80+-year-old clients. They come through the door and they always tell me the same thing: "my muscles have wasted". In response to this, I say the same thing to everyone: "Not to the extent you think they have, your body just won't let you create that much force for protection reasons".

In the UK, one in three accident and emergency visits for the elderly are due to a fall. This is something that is becoming increasingly common in the UK. Most of my elderly clients come through the door and cannot get down on the floor. If they do manage it, they insist that they just can't get back up. Normally, it takes about forty minutes with an elderly client before they can relearn to do it again. We don't focus on strengthening their muscles and we don't exercise during this time. We just start somewhere very simple; the floor.

Most of these 80 plus year old people have not sat on the floor for some time, often for maybe twenty years! Or the last time they were on the floor, it was because of a fall and they ended up getting a hip replacement or really hurting themselves. Understandably, a lot of elderly people have bad associations with the floor. Their book of life is filled with bad emotions, traumas and beliefs associated with the floor. They may have fallen before and taken months to repair the damage that was done. Some may have friends who have fallen and have gone on to build bad associations that way. Some may simply feel weaker in their old age and fear falling and what it may lead to.

Ultimately though, their subconscious selves have become very protective. In the same way that you just became weaker without muscle wastage, elderly people's ability to generate muscle force to get up off the floor dials down to protect them. If the muscle doesn't let them get up, they can't fall and get damaged. I spend most of the session on the floor getting rid of bad associations with my older clients and personally I feel it is more effective than a strength training plan. These people are already strong, they just can't use all of their strength for protection reasons. If you ask anyone on the street what happens to an elderly person after a fall, you are greeted with pretty much the same response: "it's usually downhill from there". This is a fair assumption and to be honest, a lot of elderly folks do go downhill following a fall.

So, before I even think about exercise for this type of client, bad associations need to be removed. We may spend half an hour on the floor, on our hands and knees. We may play a game down there. Sometimes I like to go through the first couple of movements of getting up. Sometimes, I may even show someone a video of another 70+ client at the start of the session unable to get up and a video of the same person at the end of their session getting up. Most of the time you can help someone within an hour to be able to get up and down onto the floor, even after years of being unable to. Remember, beliefs, context and perceptions create powerful outputs, be that the illusion of "poor posture" or how you perceive something. Focusing solely on the physical may get some people where they want to be, but for most people it's not enough! Understanding how you protect yourself with pain when you move allows you to change the processing of inputs and ultimately, change the output to what you desire: movement without pain. A good place to start is to understand how strong the human body actually is and more importantly, to understand that a lot of what you have been told, is wrong!

The Myth of the "Weak Core"

One statement that really gets my back up is "You have pain because your core is weak". This is one of the most damaging and factually incorrect statements I've ever heard. What really makes me angry though, is the mountains of evidence to debunk this myth! But, still it keeps getting pushed!

"I have a weak core". No other words make me want to slam my face into a wall as much as these ones! If the next professional you see tells you that your pain is caused by a "weak core" then please, ask them to show you the evidence that a weak core causes back pain (there isn't any). In fact, the very word "core" is incredibly poorly defined. We do not have conscious control of our core the way we think we do. When you lift your arm up, muscles like your transverse abdominal (TVA) fire automatically, beforehand. Through research, we find that it happens before you even lift your arm. One of the great joys of human movement is that postural reflexes (like TVA activation) are started in anticipation of movement and outside influences that affect balance. What an amazing thing the body is! Movement is pre-programmed in to do everything important, automatically, in a type of movement patterning. Have you ever played darts? If you have you will know there gets to a point where you almost "will" the dart where to go. Through absorbing different sensory information, postural reflexes, repetition and many other factors, you programme your patterning movement until it becomes automatic and easy. Do you think a footballer makes sure that they have their stomach drawn in and their posture "correct" before they score a goal? Most certainly not. Practice makes perfect and the more you do something, the better you get.

One tissue that gets preached in core stability, by pretty much every person living in the Jurassic era of health care, is the elusive "Transverse Abdominals" (TVA). The TVA is the deepest of the abdominal muscles and while it does indeed play an important part in spinal stability, it works together with many other muscles (including the back) to make up the "core". However, the involvement of these muscles can change depending on the task at hand. Spinal stability is a product of many systems including bone, ligaments, muscles, and most important of all, neural control. Exercise addresses both the muscular and neural functions. The very notion of a "weak" core, can cause some very serious problems for people. Believing your core is weak can lead to "guarding", a protective response wherein you create stiffness, change how you move and potentially begin to become more sensitised to potential danger. Guarding may then lead on to more protection responses such as spasms after prolonged straining of the tissues.

If the human species was supposed to be infatuated with core training because the body was so inherently weak, then why is every single obese person, or pregnant woman, or breast cancer survivor or anyone who has ever had a hernia repair, not in terrible back pain?

During a breast reconstruction, one side of the rectus abdominals is used as a source of tissue in the reconstruction. This ultimately leaves the patient with abdominal weakness on that side. However, despite this, there is still no evidence linking this to back pain. Pregnant women go through huge body-wide changes during pregnancy including truly impressive abdominal wall elongation. Even after nine months of stretching the tissue, delivering a baby, waiting eight weeks to regain pelvic stability and for the tissues to return to normal, there would be a period of terrible spinal instability. Through studies done on this topic, there is still little evidence that spinal stability plays a part in lower back pain during pregnancy. In fact, researchers studying the effects of a cognitive-behavioural approach to pain management, compared with standard physiotherapy, found some interesting results. During the study of 869 women after child birth and during a period where the rectus abdominals had not re-shortened, the surprising result was that 635 of the woman had to be dropped from the study after making a sudden, unaided and unexpected recovery in the first week.

When it comes down to it, the cold hard truth is that you are strong, but through protection mechanisms, you can't be as strong as you want to be. However, we can change that and we can do it fairly quickly. This is what the next chapter is about, when we use movement as a catalyst for change!

Impact of Belief on Levels of Pain

Mairi: What we believe we can do really affects what we can actually do. It's called "self-efficacy belief" in psychology and it's been widely researched over the last fifty or more years. The pain you are feeling is real, not imagined or made up. What Adam and I are encouraging you to do is to change what you believe you can do, despite the pain.

The good news is that you can help yourself to think again about how strong you might actually be. If you've managed to read this far in our book, you are probably open to ideas on how to change your current situation. You've probably tried lots of things in the past, some of which may have worked for a while. It is possible to completely change your life, permanently, and shake off the fibromyalgia label once and for all. Let's look for evidence to support the belief that you might be stronger than you think!

A really good place to start is by looking at what other people who are in a similar situation to yourself might have achieved. Adam's social media pages have lots of videos, photos and stories of real people whose lives have changed forever after they took on the challenge of moving more and moving better. None of the people or stories shown are made up or exaggerated. These are real people with real health conditions who have suffered pain for years. They have got better, not because they have some super powers. Their pain and suffering is no less than other people with similar conditions. They have just decided to take control of their lives, to try their best to make the changes that have been recommended and to keep doing them, every day, for the rest of their lives. Ask yourself, can you do the same? Might it be possible that you could also do what you need to in order to get better? Of course, there will be good days and bad days; that's life after all! It will hurt at times and you'll be frustrated, sometimes angry and occasionally disappointed, but tomorrow is another day. Have a look at the articles which tell you a bit about the people behind the transformations. Maybe some of their experiences will sound familiar to you and you'll see part of your own story in theirs. If they can do it and you can see proof of their change, you can do the same. Maybe one day your story will be up there to inspire and motivate somebody who is just like you now!

We all know that it's important to set goals for your improvement but think about what those goals could actually be. Don't sell yourself short here! Yes, it's important to take small steps towards improvement and believe me, it feels great when you've achieved that first small victory! Breaking down the challenge into bite size chunks is a good idea, but don't lose sight of the main target. I remember the first day I met Adam, he asked me to have a go at flipping the tractor tyre he had lying in the middle of the studio. I remember looking and thinking "don't be ridiculous!". That morning I had cried with pain when lifting my laptop up, so bending my knees, grabbing hold of a tractor tyre and flipping it fully over was impossible, as far as I could see. But Adam smiled and nodded and told me how to use the strength that I had and move the way my body was designed to and have a go. Thankfully, my response was captured on video and the excitement and joy that shone from my face when the tyre flipped over was caught on film for all to see. I did it! I thought that it's not possible and yet, I did it! Back home afterwards and a few days later, I wondered if I might be able to take my dog for a walk round the woods, a three-mile round trip. I messaged Adam to ask him if he thought it might be possible and he told me not to ask if it's possible but to tell myself it was definitely going to happen. Off we went and sure enough, 45 minutes later a tired, sweaty but very happy Mairi (and slobbery dog) returned from the walk, delighted to have made my body transport me further than it had in more than ten years. I'm no different from anyone else with fibromyalgia. My pain and fatigue was real and disabling, but now it's gone. It's up to me how much I make of life now and how fit I become, but you have the same choice open to you. It's up to you what you make of it.

I'll admit, there were days when I thought about curling up in bed and not facing the stretches and movements that Adam prescribed for me. Then the excuses would appear in my mind in rapid fire succession. I'm too busy, I have an appointment to keep, I'm expecting an electrician, there's no space to move around in my house, the list goes on and on. I would intend to prioritise everything before allowing myself the time to do the work needed to get better. This, of course, makes no sense but I would continue to argue with myself to avoid the things I didn't want to do. I would say to myself, well you see I have low self-esteem so that's why I put my own needs last and everyone else's, including complete strangers, deserve more of my efforts than I'm willing to invest in my own wellbeing. What a load of bollocks that is! If I have enough self-awareness to give myself permission to not do something because I'm not feeling worthy my self-talk has become out of control! If making excuses ever becomes an Olympic sport, I could be a gold medal winner for my country. Sometimes, you have to give yourself a bit of tough love to just get up and get on with what needs done. Remind yourself that a better you will be a better partner, son or daughter, parent, friend and so on, if you try to use the low self-esteem card to dodge what you need to do. You'll be a better low self-esteem server of others/victim/doormat if you make the changes that will improve your health so do it for them if not for yourself! Take the time to think about what excuses you are making to yourself which are holding you back and see if you can come up with a counter argument. It will become a battle of minds with yourself but you can help yourself by being aware of what's standing in your way and prioritising getting well above the everyday barriers that try to get in your way.

Part Three

Magic Movement

Adam: So, this is surely where I reveal some patented, elusive, oddly omnipotent, and don't forget expensive exercise right? And it can be yours, all yours, for only five easy instalments of £99.99. Well, sorry to disappoint you, but if you assume this you would be wrong! The cold hard, shocking truth, is that there is no secret exercise, there is no special way to move and definitely don't be fooled by anyone monetising the situation and stating that there is!

Have you ever looked at humans? We come in all sorts of crazy shapes and sizes, we have different levers, we have different centres of mass dependant on our height and even our gender! Some of us are great at certain exercises and movements, but we suck at others. However, our friends and family might suck at the exercises we are good at and outperform us in the ones that we find hard. The point I'm trying to make is that people are different, in absolutely every sense of the word. There is no single magic exercise or movement, it simply does not exist. Whatever movement you choose to do, it has always been and forever will be, an input. If you process a certain movement, let's say spinal flexion, and subconsciously deem it necessary to create a protection output, because perhaps years ago, some archaic doctor told you that you had a slipped disc. Then guess what happens when you bend over to pick up your shopping at the weekend and actually go into spinal flexion? Yup, you guessed it, a lot of pain to say "Hey, we need to avoid this movement, it's bad for us". Over time, this message will therefore get reinforced and you will end up avoiding bending over completely.

Earlier on, we touched on lower back pain and the various and plentiful "core" exercises that are used worldwide. We know through mountains of research that it's simply the movement that helps people with lower back pain and not the specialized core exercises. In fact, pretty much any exercise is just as effective for lower back pain. We have the data! Yet a quick internet search for core exercises will yield mountains of inaccurate information on the subject and even more gadgets, gizmos and DVD's you can buy to "strengthen your core". So, even though the "weak core" theory for things like back pain has been debunked for nearly a decade, why is it so deeply ingrained in our society? Well, the answer is simple. It's hard to change people's minds when their livelihoods depend on it! Imagine being a brilliant posture specialist, a misalignment expert or even a "core" guru and then suddenly, the mechanisms as to how you think your treatment work get debunked by new research. Keep in mind that people spend thousands of pounds over their career on various different courses and tools for their professions. In such a state of inner turmoil and cognitive dissonance, "specialists" will find a confirmation bias to help cling onto their old ways and unfortunately, it doesn't work out too well for everyone else's bank accounts. Now, don't get me wrong, that's not every specialist. There are mountains of therapists abandoning the old manual therapy ways and moving into a more BPS friendly space. The paradigm is shifting, albeit slowly. Look at chiropractors for example. We see small numbers who are now throwing out the old "spinal subluxation" theory because of lack of evidence. These specialists are growing as professionals, helping more people, all whilst helping their patients achieve self-sufficiency. I'm not saying these modalities or ways of doing things don't work, as, clearly, in a lot of cases they do. It's just that they don't work for the reason we think they do. After all, anything someone does to you or any exercise you participate in, gadgets you buy or the oils you take, are all inputs. However, it's how that input is processed that dictates how well that treatment, modality or exercise will work for you. This is why one treatment may work for one person, but not another.

Take for example getting a massage. I love getting a massage after a stressful week or two. It's half an hour lying down in a dimly lit room, no stress, no kids and for half an hour, nothing really matters any more. Just talking about it makes want to go and book one! However, we know that it's impossible to release muscles or for that tiny massage therapist's hands to release my fascia. However, some of the buzz words surrounding massage like "release muscles" or my personal favourite "work those trigger points", we know are just not physically possible. Did you know there isn't actually any real "credible" evidence to suggest trigger points even exist, in fact there's probably more evidence to such "Big foot" is real" but that topic is probably a whole other book right there!

Right about now you're probably thinking "Well if you can't release muscle tension, then why are you going?" and my answer is what I hope anyone's answer would be. Not only for massage, but any treatment! I will go for a fortnightly massage because it does do something.

I have a good relationship with my massage therapist, she's my friend and I trust her. I'm also a human and as such crave human contact and touch. My massage therapist isn't releasing my muscles, but she is doing something. She provides a safe environment, therapeutic alliance, touch and ultimately an input to my nervous system. She isn't treating trigger points, she's touching my brain through my nervous system, through my skin. If you gave me a massage on a Monday and again on a Wednesday, we used the same therapist, used the same treatment bed, it was at the same time, let's say 2pm and we even did it in the same room, then I can guarantee I will enjoy the Wednesday massage way more! On Mondays I work until 6pm, but on Wednesdays I take a half day and finish at 1pm. This very slight detail changes how I process my massage input, as on the Monday I can't fully relax because I know I need to go back to work. However, for Wednesday's massage I have already finished work beforehand. I have no commitments and I know I can just truly relax.

I've received the same input on both days, but how the input (massage) is processed is completely different and as such, creates a different output. If I don't have to go back to work, my brain almost gives my body permission to fully relax. Remember, it's your brain that tells your muscle to relax, not somebody's hands. This is also true for exercise and movement. Whatever you do is going to be an input and it is how it's processed that decides what you get out of it. If your next-door neighbour Lucy has had a bad back for 20 years, one day signs up for a new Pilates class at the local gym and is suddenly doing back flips in her garden and now says she feels great, then there's a very good chance you are going to find that class just as beneficial. However, it's not the exercise, it's the anticipation, perception and processing of the input that yields the results. If you have seen Lucy try everything for her back and nothing has worked, yet now she's doing great because of the class, then that's going to go into your book of life and influence how you process that Pilates class. Your body is capable, it is already strong and it doesn't need expensive, complicated exercises to help you get better.

I will always be biased towards using movement as the catalyst for change, after all, that's what helped me. I feel movement is a great way to not only improve how you feel physically, but to improve how you feel emotionally and socially too, as they all influence each other. When you become able to do a shopping trip without pain, you feel great after the retail therapy. When you have booked to go out with your friends and don't have to cancel at the last minute, you feel great socially and emotionally. Using movement as the catalyst for change is a great way influence the Biopsychosocial you, inexpensively and you know, as crazy as its sounds....it can even be fun.

Unhelpful Associations

Mairi: Starting to get a life after so long watching from the sidelines is amazing, but it's also quite terrifying. Frustratingly, it's not just as simple as picking up where you left off when the pain began to kick in and limited your activity. If you're anything like me, you will have had loads of setbacks over the years. Things that were previously easy to do became a challenge and I'm sure there were lots of times when, no matter how hard you tried, you weren't able to do things as well as you had in your pre-fibro days. For me, this was a huge blow to my (already low) self-esteem and getting my confidence back was not going to happen overnight. Getting back to my pre-fibro days seemed like it was probably going to take a while, but I was happy to be able to have the opportunity to take on the challenge! There is probably a whole other book to be written on how to break the link between bad experiences and their impact on a person, and I'm not sure that I'm qualified to write that one just yet! Having said that, I think it's important to think about the challenges you will face and how you might tackle them. The best thing I can do to help, I think, is to give an example of one of my challenges and how I faced it.

The example I'm going to write about is getting back into work. Before my health got really bad, I was a psychology lecturer in a university. I loved my job but my health made me quite unreliable as an employee. I kept pushing myself to do the job as soon as I felt a bit better, but this would only make my symptoms worse. I had got myself into a crash and burn cycle and my confidence and mental health were really low. I was working in a specific area which I knew quite a bit about in theory, but I was teaching student nurses. I knew little about the job of the mental health nurse and had no relevant experience of adult nursing so there was a real element of pushing the boundaries of my experience.

My track record with work has been tricky since my health worsened. Most people were understanding and supportive but in a previous job, I had a really unpleasant experience. I'm pretty sure my employer didn't believe there was anything really wrong with me and they certainly didn't offer any support for my condition. In fact, the opposite was true. I was given jobs to do that were beyond my knowledge or experience with no support and I was told if I couldn't do it, there was plenty of people looking for a job who could. I was even given the job as the fire warden! Why would you give a person with mobility issues the task of being the last to leave a building when the fire alarm goes off, when the lifts were switched off and expect them to check every room to make sure everybody else has got out safely? Along with this, my list of tasks was regularly changed at the last minute, meaning I had little time to prepare for what I was expected to do and the work that I had done to prepare for what I had previously expected to do was no longer needed. It was made clear to me that I was personally disliked and distrusted and the whole toxic mess contributed significantly to making me anxious and distressed when trying to do my job.

This is a significant chapter for me in what Adam calls my Book of Life. My confidence in my ability to do an academic job had been crushed and when I have the opportunity now to support a student at the university, I become fearful and anxious about what might happen next. There is a kind of internal voice which provides a running commentary of our thoughts. To help explain my thought process, I'm going to describe the thoughts as if it was a conversation which I hope will make it understandable.

First, I'm starting with a body scan of how I physically feel at the prospect of starting back at work. My stomach is the first place I notice the anxiety and I think I have a tightness in my chest too. So, this tells me that I am anxious and a bit scared about making a start on the job. My immediate response is to hope that the student has cancelled the appointment – I guess in terms in fight or flight that would be the flight option! Having checked my emails, no such luck, the appointment remains in place. This is a good thing because I firmly believe that avoidance is bad. If I avoid meeting up with the student, the anxiety will remain and the next time I have a chance to get back to work, it's going to be just as much of an ordeal. The only way to change the situation is by facing it and hopefully changing the outcome.

The next step for me is to try to work out what is causing the stress for me. What is it exactly that I'm worried about? Specifically, what is my worst-case scenario for this meeting? The first thing that springs to mind is that I won't be able to help the student and I will let them down. This would seem likely to me since my confidence is low and my ability to support a student has been questioned in the past. But if my employer thought this was the case, they wouldn't let me do the job. I haven't let students down in the past to the best of my knowledge. I want to help and know what the students usually need. The evidence, therefore, suggests that this fear is unfounded.

Quick body scan. Stomach churning. Feeling sick. Headache starting. Time for a cup of tea and some slow breathing.

What if the student doesn't like me? What if they go out of their way to give me a hard time or set traps to show that I'm rubbish? Well it's possible they may not become my best friend but I'm a tutor not a befriender. I'm there to do a job providing academic support. I'll do it to the best of my ability and I'll try to be polite and friendly when I do it. In my experience, that's usually what the students do too. They are hoping for the same end result as me. If they chose to be grumpy that's up to them. If it upsets me I can ask to be reallocated. But I don't realistically expect that to happen.

And so, it goes on and on. In the run up to doing something new or something that I haven't done for a while there is a running commentary in my head of possible catastrophic outcomes. For each one I unpick the thoughts to try to work out what the actual thing I'm worried about is. I then weigh up the evidence for and against. Is this outcome likely based on my experience? What can I do to try to limit the things that might go wrong? What are the potential positive outcomes of going through with this thing? I think this is a time for being kind to ourselves when trying to recognise and challenge unhelpful associations. They have been built up over a lifetime and won't just disappear overnight. I would say again, though, that avoidance is bad. It's usually better to have a go, prepare beforehand as well as you can and review afterwards. What went well and what could you do differently next time. It sounds so simple in theory but in practice, it takes time and perseverance. Part of getting better is improving your emotional health as well as your physical strength, so it's important to keep these mental workouts as part of your road to recovery! I'm guessing, the more you do the challenging stuff, the easier it gets over time. Sounds like a plan to me.

Pie

Adam: Now that we know there is no magic way to move and that essentially every movement and exercise is an input, where do we start? Well, your body is perfectly capable of high impact exercises like aerobics. You also have enough muscle mass to flip a big 100kg tractor tyre, and if you really wanted to, you could create your own programme. These are all possible with the body you have right now. However, I would not suggest you start here. Although you are capable and there is no perfect way to move, you do need to be introduced back into movement in a productive way. This will ensure you don't hit a wall, cause a flare up or simply lose motivation. I've said it a thousand times already with clients and I'm sure I'll be saying it many more times in the years to come "I want you training smarter than everyone else, not harder". So, this is what this chapter is about, it's about being smarter. A huge part of training smarter is to understand the power of movement and that first step is to understand the power of your Pie!

I'm slightly sad that I won't get to see the expression on your face as you read that last sentence, most people look at me really confused! Thinking of yourself as Pie will help you begin to understand how movement can be a catalyst for profound change.

At the end of the day we are all humans, but today, let's think of ourselves as pie charts and the slices that we consist of are Physical, Psychological and Social. Each slice represents Biopsychosocial factors that can influence how we experience chronic pain and ultimately, how we move. You may have a huge slice of pie that is Physical, with perhaps a little slice of Psychological and a little slice of Social. So, you could be someone with Rheumatoid arthritis (Physical), who manages it incredibly well (Psychological) and also someone who enjoys a good drink with friends and family regularly (Social). But then again, you could have a tiny Physical slice, a huge Psychological slice and a huge Social slice. So, you could be someone who in the past had a damaged leg that healed, but the pain never turned off. Technically, the physical inputs that drive your pain are relatively small (Physical). But being in pain for so long is more than likely going to bring along depression at some point (Psychological) and obviously with being depressed and in constant pain all the time, it's going to negatively influence the things you do during the day (Social). Even your gender may be a factor. In our society the mentality that "Boys are not supposed to cry" is still rampant and as such, it is the reason why we have so many men is pain, suffering in silence. People have different slices, after all, we are each unique. We have different past histories and a subjective view of the world. However, the point to take home is that every single person has a slice of all three. You cannot be just Physical or just Physical and Social, everyone reading this is difference slices of all three.

Ok, I'm starting to get hungry now with all this talk of pie, so let's explain why understanding your Pie is important. The things we do during the day, whether they are Physical things like a walk to the shops, Psychological things, like the flood of feel good chemicals you get when finding out the dog that always chases you when you go to the shops has no teeth or a Social thing like spending time with your friends. Whatever it is you do, Physical, Psychological or Social, it does not just affect that slice of the pie, but it effects the other two. It is because of this that I chose movement as my catalyst for getting out of pain. I personally feel there is no other modality that is as powerful at affecting the other slices of pie as movement.

Years ago, I would avoid a big shopping centre in my home town. But, every so often I would be forced to visit it. I would walk a hundred meters or so and the impact of my feet striking the shopping centre floor would aggravate my neck and cause it to ache unrelentingly. I would find a little bench that was meant for the elderly or people with disabilities and I'd sit down for a few minutes, or longer, just until the pain subsided and I felt ready to walk again. This Physical act of not being able to walk very far would impact my Psychological slice, as I'd sit there with individuals 60+ years my senior who were all rubbing their painful feet. Only a year previous I had been patrolling miles every day with heavy equipment strapped to my back, driving tanks and fighting In Afghanistan. To now be sat down with the elderly because I couldn't walk more than 100 meters without pain, it didn't feel very nice and it slowly seeped into my Psychological slice and affected how I felt on a day to day basis. I would think, what's the point of even being here anymore, if I couldn't even walk around a shopping centre. This obviously affected my Social slice as I didn't want to participate in social activities. A good example was my friend Jon's stag do. One of the party games on the stag do was to be dragged around a lake in a rubber ring attached to a speed boat. I wanted so badly to join in and It felt truly awful watching from the side as everyone enjoyed themselves, yet I couldn't participate because I didn't want to aggravate my neck.

I fondly remember the day I was in this shopping centre again, time was against me, I had to pick up some essentials before I had to survive a shift at work. I eventually got everything I needed. I had walked fast around the centre and hadn't really been taking much notice of anything as I was so busy. Just as I was on the way out, I saw them, I saw the three people who made me realise what I had just done. As I walked out the shops, three elderly ladies were sitting on a bench eating pastries, massaging their tired 70 something legs. It was truly a magnificent revelation for me! Watching these little old ladies, I suddenly realised I had just walked for 30 minutes without interruption, no neck ache, no bad back, no feeling weak sat on a bench. The next day I decided to go back to the shopping centre, but this time with no time limit and no fear of pain from walking, I walked a full 45 minutes around that shopping centre with my headphones in just smiling. I browsed the shops for as long as I wanted because I didn't have to sit down, I sat and ate a donut and watched people walk by, but by far my favourite part of that day was when I walked down to the arcades and I bought a token for the bumper cars. If you had been in that arcade that day, you may just have seen the happiest man in the world to ever drive a bumper car. A simple change in my Physical slice had dramatically changed my Psychological slice as I walked around the shopping centre in the best mood I'd been in for a long time. As I bought items from the shops, I would smile and talk to the people serving me, instead of giving them my infamous stoic face and short pain fuelled sentences. This one Physical act of being able to walk more than 100 meters changed how I felt. It changed how I talked to people and more importantly, it changed my outputs to the ones I would create before Afghanistan. I felt like I had a purpose again and that purpose was solely to get better. I often say to people "You can either be interested in recovery, or you can be committed, but you can't be both" and that day is the day that I became committed.

In the early days of creating my programme, I truly realised just how powerful movement could be. I had spent a lot of time breaking down the beliefs about my "weak neck" and I had done more research than you could shake a stick at! I eventually began to introduce graded high impact work into my own daily movements. Normally, even just thinking about these kinds of movements would have set my neck off into to a week long flare up. However, doing short bursts every day was allowing me to break down my old beliefs about my neck. I soon found I could go for longer and longer each day with the movements. Each session slowly convinced my subconscious that this movement was safe, that I was safe, that I didn't need protecting. The more I researched and the more I realised that I wasn't going to damage my neck, the better it felt. Something strange happens when you stop producing pain and it's not something you would really expect. When you stop producing pain, nothing happens. You don't get an immediate Eureka moment and get to bask in the glory of being pain free. You don't suddenly get alerted that its gone, you literally get nothing. You don't even realise the change has happened. You have read the entire last paragraph and completely forgotten about how you can always feel the weight of your shirt on your shoulders, but now you can feel it. You didn't realise you can always see your nose, no matter where you look and now you have noticed it again. You may have put a watch on this morning, felt it on your wrist for 20 seconds and then never felt it again until I've just mentioned it, until we bring your consciousness back to it. We get so many inputs every single day and our brain and spinal cord work together to block out the ones that are not important. But, when they deem it is important, it doesn't get blocked and the input gets an open invite straight to the brain to process the input. It was actually my partner who first realised my neck was better, when we were standing in a queue at the cinema. She turned to me and said, "You know, you haven't mentioned your neck in a very long time. How is it?" I was a little confused at first, as I didn’t really know what she was talking about. But then I thought about it and I was fine; my neck was fine. I hadn't actually given it much thought in months. Little bit by little bit, I had re-written the chapter about my neck in my book of life and not even realised it. This was my eventual Eureka moment.

So, if you are going to commit to using movement as your recovery tool, you must respect how powerful it is. As you can see from my little story, it has the power to be your best friend or it can be you worst enemy. Right now, it's your enemy. Like all great generals, we need to learn everything we can about the enemy, so that we can take on the challenge and ultimately defeat them!

Pre-Foundation

Adam: If you're reading this book then there is a good chance you have already tried to exercise before and it was more than likely at the advice of your general practitioner. I hear this a lot from people. They get diagnosed and are told to go away and exercise, and when they do it causes a huge flare up. Exercise then remains something that is seldom re-visited. I'm going to take a hard-calculated guess and say it didn't work out too well for you, right? Don't worry about it, you are not alone. Like all things that we do to ourselves, exercise is just another input. The input can be the same for everyone, but how it's processed that dictates what output we get. You tried to exercise, Subconscious You deemed it to dangerous and decided to create an output to condition you to not do it again. As far as your brain is concerned, this is a tactic that works, so doing it over and over again is a good way to keep you safe. Making you hurt for days afterward stops you from exercising and if it works, your brain will keep following this strategy. There are many reasons why you created this output in the first place and we have talked about a lot of them in the previous chapters. However, if we are going to get a new, positive output from exercise, then we need to eliminate some of the more likely reasons why a negative output was created.

Lots of research and evidence is available now that suggests a very simply reason as to why we have a brain in the first place and that reason is movement. We need a brain to help use past experiences, beliefs and everything else in that book of life to predict possible future outcomes and allow us to navigate safely through the world. Our brain helps us to understand how our actions will affect the environment around us and ourselves. If you look at the small sea squirt creature, you will find that in its early years it uses its brain to help swim around, that is, until it eventually latches on to something stationary where it will live out the rest of its life. Once its attached it starts to eat its own brain for food. Without the need for movement, there isn’t really much need for a brain. Being stationary is far safer than moving around in the world and having a brain is nothing more than excess for our little sea squirt friend, especially when he can't interact with the environment around him. So, with that in mind, think about how much danger your brain may perceive when just walking to the shops, compared to that very same walk when the ground is covered in ice from three days' worth of snow. How much more do you think you would protect yourself, with the knowledge that falling is much more likely? How much more protective do you think 90-year-old Doris would be, given the fact that she knows one out of every three admissions to accident and emergency for the elderly are because of a fall. Again, same inputs, different outputs, depending on how they are processed. Movement is a glorious thing, but it comes with inherent danger and when you live in chronic pain, that potential danger gets magnified. Normally, your body deals with danger in a fight or flight manner, but what happens when your own brain thinks that you aren’t equipped to deal with either? That's simple. It tries to stop you moving. After all, if you don’t leave the house, you aren’t in as much danger, right? Our task here and now is to change how you perceive movement and/or exercise at a subconscious level, thus helping you to turn the input (movement) into a positive output (feel good chemicals and no pain).

I want you to forget about exercise for a moment. It is after all, a stupid word, a social construct or whatever else you want to call it.

You will already have a lot of negative associations with that word and what it personally means to you, so let's kill that right now. As you move onto the first step of your recovery "the foundation phase", we aren't going to be exercising. We are definitely not going to be jumping around or doing things that are incredibly hard or too taxing. However, what we are going to be doing, is creating a solid foundation upon which to build your strength.

When you build a house on sand, every brick laid is just as weak as the one laid before it. This is because the foundation is weak, its unstable and it was also a very bad idea right from the beginning. Ask any builder and they will tell you we don't build houses on sand! So then, why would we build ourselves up from an unstable foundation? The first part of putting everything into practice, reintroducing movement and getting rid of pain, is to create a solid foundation.

Building your foundation

Wellness is Your Absolute Priority

Adam: When It comes to building your foundation, we need it to be built from aspects of the Biological, the Psychological and the Social world. After all, we are Biopsychosocial beings. We want a consistently strong foundation to build upon. We want it to be a well-rounded, multi-disciplined and most importantly, for the next two weeks, it needs to be your absolute priority: what you eat, sleep and breathe. Get through the foundation phase and you are 50% of the way to wellness. Everything else becomes much easier after you've done the foundation work. This is the hard part, the changing of routine, the trying of new things, but for the next two weeks, you ARE a lean mean strength building machine!

The foundation phase is going to take you two weeks to complete. We are going to be changing a lot of how you process the Physical, Psychological and Social aspects of your life that affect you as an individual. Your foundation phase is a way to reintroduce movement in a safe and non-threatening way by starting off at a level you have control of. It allows you to build a routine, condition yourself, create new habits and over a period of a few weeks, you will see how the movements that were initially hard in the beginning, become increasingly much easier. All of this will help reinforce that it's the processing that matters and not the movements (inputs). This will help you to see how inherently strong you are and, more importantly, how Bioplastic you are. You have ended up in your current situation through a whole combination of complicated adaptations, so rest assured that you can once again adapt, but this time in your favour. Our foundation phase needs to be done every day. That means no "oh I don't feel like it today", no "I'm in pain" and certainly no, "I can't do it". Anyone that knows me will tell you the "C" word, is strictly prohibited in my studio. That's the word "can't" by the way – just for the avoidance of doubt. You do not need to do everything 100% correctly, sometimes you can mess the order up and get away with it, but under no circumstance, stray from consistency.

If you eat McDonalds today for dinner, you will look the same in the mirror tomorrow as you did today. If you eat McDonalds tomorrow and the day after for dinner, you will look the same in the mirror then as you did today. However, eat it every day and I can't tell you when, but at some point, the consistency of eating them every day for dinner will make you gain weight and you will see someone else in that mirror.

Your recovery ahead, your journey, it isn't going to be made up of some big empowering speech where something profound happens at the end of it, nor is it going to consist of doing one specific thing and ultimately everything all comes together nice and easy. Your journey consists of you waking up every day, consistently doing everything you need to do that day and understanding that this isn't going to be linear and that life is going to try and get in the way. But, to succeed you need to push on regardless and remember why you started this journey in the first place. Your journey is not one of motivation, but of self-discipline. If you want something you have never had before, you must do what you have never done before. We are going to spend this chapter covering each component that will make up your foundation phase before moving on to the next chapter and putting them all into practice.

Mairi: I don't know about you but when I heard this from Adam, my immediate response to choosing wellness as my absolute priority was that I would love that to happen, but.... He's heard that before countless times. My priority was and still is my family. If I prioritised what he was going to ask me to do, would it impact negatively on them? Would I not be able to do the little bit of parenting that I was currently managing? What about the risks? Would I end up making myself worse, causing a huge flare up of pain and fatigue? Was I being selfish and irresponsible in making a decision to, as Adam say, eat, sleep and breathe the foundation building?

Actually, the opposite was true. By prioritising my move to wellness, I was being selfless and highly responsible. I was making the decision to take control of my health and to change it for the better. In doing so, I have regained movement and a level of fitness I never thought possible. This has allowed me to do things with and for my family that I wouldn't previously have dreamed of. My family has a far healthier mum, wife and daughter than they would have had if I hadn't prioritised the Foundation Building that Adam advised. We've talked about it many times since I took the plunge and we are unanimous: it was the best two weeks' investment I ever made.

Wake Up, Shake Up and Stay Up

Adam: Just like Mairi said earlier, procrastination is not your friend. For the most part it will do nothing but rob you of your most precious resource: time. Your journey needs a powerful start, something that will completely change your day and kick start new habits and patterns of thinking. The first thing we must do is to create a fresh start to our day. Chances are you stick to the same routines that you have done for months. It's only natural, we are after all creatures of habit. But, like I said before, if you do the same things every day, then expect to have the same results. On day one of your foundations you are going to do something that goes against all your beliefs and which is probably something you would normally avoid. I am talking of course about showering cold. A new input for a new journey.

Cold Showers

Before you dive head first into cold showering it's important to assess your individual situation and please do consult your GP. If you have a pre-existing heart problem or a lung condition it may be worth skipping the cold showers or at least introducing them in a very graded manner.

I have used cold showers for around six years and you can regularly catch me swimming in the sea on a crisp December morning, here in the northeast of England. Cold water is a powerful driver for change, it is also accessible to most and is a fantastic way to push that Bioplasticity that we talked about earlier. Cold showering forces surface vessels to vasoconstrict and directs oxygen-rich blood deeper into the body towards organs as a way to conserve heat. Cold water also releases pain killing noradrenaline and floods your system with many rewarding feel-good chemicals like dopamine. There is a strange sense of achievement after finishing your first cold shower and it is a tried and tested method that helps to create a new type of day to embark on. It puts you back in control. Control is what I want you to gain in the foundation phase. Your active participation in the treatment of your chronic pain will yield a much better outcome than if you were simply passive. It's also important to remember that your brain can turn nerves up and down whenever it feels this is in your best interest. By exposing ourselves to a blast of cold water first thing on a morning, you will find it will greatly help to shush down your nerves and in doing so, make them less sensitive. This will help to condition you both physically to oxidative stress and psychologically by getting over your initial fear. I like to think fear stands for "false evidence appearing real". Right now, a cold shower probably fills you with fear, but once it's done, you will feel pretty good about yourself and be able to see that the false evidence you held that made you reluctant to try them, was indeed just that, false. So, when day one comes around, get in your shower, wash as normal with hot water and then gradually turn the temperature down. Once you hit the cold, stay with it for two minutes and don't forget to breathe! Around three years ago I began to tell potential clients to cold shower for seven days after their initial consultation. Many people did not come back because of this. They simply were not ready to expose themselves to that level of stress or change, but the ones that did have gone on to do incredibly things and have completely change their lives. A common thing I hear is "Just showering takes it out of me for the rest of the day" and this will be true, but this is probably due to the warm temperature of the water. Cold water is entirely different however. You should expect to get out of the shower with more energy than when you got in, refreshed and holding a certain level of accomplishment that you didn't previously hold that morning. This is your first step and it's an important one. Many have done it before you and many will do it after you. The first step is the hardest.

Mairi: When Adam first suggested that I take a cold shower for two minutes every morning I thought he must be truly crazy. I could not think of anything worse at that point. I couldn't even stand for long enough to have a normal shower but standing under cold water? For two minutes?? The very thought was enough to bring on a flare up of pain. Surely it would be agony? Warm water in the bath was soothing but cold water must inevitably cause my muscles to contract and get tighter and the pain must be unbearable if this happens. I honestly couldn't imagine anything that would cause more agony than the very thing he was suggesting I do to help relieve pain. However, I'd paid my money and had his advice so there was nothing else for it. The next day I staggered into the shower, performed my ablutions, turned the dial to the blue setting and braced myself for impact. A very strange falsetto wail spontaneously erupted from me and it was definitely a bit of a shock to the system, that's for sure. Truthfully, I didn't manage two full minutes but the cold water did cover me completely. Adam had said I had to do it long enough to get to the "oooooh" sharp intake of breath stage. I got there pretty quickly and exited the bathroom sharpish.

Still making some very strange noises, I dried and dressed myself. I was in such a hurry to get dressed that I didn't even have time to think about how I was feeling but once clothed and warmed up, I did a body scan to see what was hurting this particular morning. My legs were a bit stiff, not the worst I'd ever had by a long way. But the searing agony that I was expecting was not happening. I thanked my lucky stars and put thoughts of tomorrow's repeat performance out of my mind.

As the day wore on, my pain was definitely none the worse for the morning ordeal. In fact, if anything, I felt it had eased slightly. One thing that was definitely better was my fatigue level. I actually didn't feel the crushing exhaustion that comes with the fibro diagnosis. I had a short sleep in the afternoon but by the evening time, I was still reasonably alert. One thing I remember well is that I slept better that night than I had in a long time.

The next day I repeated the ordeal, including the automatic yodelling that brought noisy complaints from the children. I wouldn't say day two was any easier than day one but there was still no flare up afterwards. By day two I was starting to reduce my pain meds so any increase in pain would have been very noticeable. Again, I noticed that my fatigue levels were less and reluctantly, I decided to continue with this horrible therapy. By the end of the first week, I was completely free of pain relief medications. The showers were absolutely no less awful but I was finally getting into a normal routine for sleep and coping with a normal day without exhaustion. I had also started to notice a shift in my mood with less depression and anxiety hanging around in the background. Surely there must be a mistake? I'd been treated for depression for years. I'd even done a PhD in trauma psychology for fecks sake! If a cold shower was a useful treatment for either fibromyalgia or any mental health issues, how was it that I hadn't come across it before now?

I sat down and decided to search for anything that had been studied about the beneficial effects of cold showers on pain, fatigue and mental health conditions. My searches found almost nothing except a few small-scale studies published in some obscure academic journals. This told me that cold showers for treating the conditions I was interested in was not widely researched. Scientific researchers don't give up as easily as that, though, and I decided to look for other ways that the idea might have been studied. I came across a treatment called cryotherapy which is an experience where a person sits in an open cabin and gets blasted with air cooled with nitrogen to given them a controlled low temperature full body experience. "Sounds absolutely appalling" I thought, so that was the avenue I chose, of course! And as it turns out, cryotherapy has been tested as a possible treatment for fibromyalgia and has been under research for nearly forty years!

Researchers have tested this cold therapy treatment in people diagnosed with fibromyalgia as well as rheumatoid arthritis, osteoarthritis, chronic low back pain and various other chronic pain conditions. When these people spent two and half minutes in the cold cabin, they rated a significant decrease in their pain symptoms afterwards. Some people found the effect didn't last long (about 90 minutes) but many found an ongoing improvement over time. This fits with my own experience, where I combined the cold showers with increasing levels of movement, bringing my pain levels down to nil.

I carried out more searches of research databases and I found that cold therapy had been widely tested on a number of chronic pain conditions and was regularly used to treat muscle fatigue in elite athletes. I recalled having seen one of Scotland's top sportsmen sitting in a bath of ice after a tournament and this sealed the deal for me! I was disappointed that there hasn't been more research done on this simple and cheap therapy which could help so many people if it was found to be useful and I started to consider why this might be. The obvious first objection is going to be from the patient who has this therapy recommended to them as they will probably be pretty reluctant to take on the idea in any form! But I did it, so other people need to know that it might be effective to give them the opportunity to consider it. I was pretty desperate and was prepared to try anything that might have taken away some of the pain I was in, so I think it's only fair that other consenting adults should be given the chance to try this. Of course, if it works, it would mean a significant reduction in pain relief consumption so surely this is a positive for our overstretched health service? It may be that there are issues around the cold-water treatment that we don't know about yet. Perhaps the shock would be too much for some people or maybe if an undiagnosed heart condition was present, there would be an obvious risk to doing this. I would urge anyone to consider it, having first checked with their medial professional to rule out any risks that the cold water might carry for them. Otherwise, I can't recommend it highly enough as an effective, drug free natural treatment for chronic pain, fatigue and depression.

I want to end this chapter with a hypothesis about why this treatment might work. This is "world according to Mairi" blue sky thinking, but there is some evidence from peer reviewed published research that backs up these ideas. A possible reason why cold water might help to relieve pain is that it releases a shot of feel-good hormones like beta-endorphin and noradrenaline. This may be enough to shock the nervous system out of the pain cycle, in a similar way to the Electroconvulsive therapy is used to treat drug-resistant depression. If any researchers out there would like to test this theory and extend its use if successful, I'd be happy to share the list of articles I have that have begun the lengthy process of evaluating the therapy. It would be great to see this potentially beneficial therapy make a difference in a lot of people's lives so if you have a mind to do so, please do go ahead and take this theory further!

Everyday Movement

Adam: Like I said previously, we are not going to be exercising, we are going to be moving, the two are worlds apart! Exercise has a lot of bad association for those in chronic pain and movement is something you will already do, it's just a little difficult at the moment.

The movement part of our Foundation phase, in my opinion, is the one that is the most important. Regular movement will help to introduce a routine and you will see that it become easier, the more you do. The easier it becomes, the more confident you will become with your movement. The more confident you feel with movement, the more stable you will feel. The more stable you feel, the more mobility your brain will allow. I've said before that speed hides a need for something and you can see this a lot with movement. If someone tends to protect a specific leg, perhaps one which has had a knee replacement, then you can bet they won't spend as much time on that leg and when they walk, effectively speed through the movement on that side. Our bodies are great at compensating and sometimes when we feel we lack stability, the brain cuts back on how much mobility we can have. Things like balance can be a huge reason for you brain to cut your mobility allowance. However, balance isn't something that can just be trained, it's a product of many systems: muscle, proprioception, neural control, the vestibular system, etc., all working together. As you follow your foundation exercises you will find that your balance improves automatically. This is not because you have been training your balance, it's just the systems that work together to produce it are now working much better together.

Trying to explain certain movements in written form can be somewhat difficult and sometimes even pictures are not enough. Because of this, Mairi and myself opened the "No Pain, No Pain" private section on my website. In here you will find video explanations of all the movements described in the book, from the sample foundation movements, to a neat little video on counter-rotation when you walk. To access the private part visit www.thefibroguy.com, click on the side link "No Pain, No Pain private" and enter the password "NOPAIN88".

Sensory Turn Downs

The first movements I want you to start with are stretches and it isn't going to be for the reasons you think. Everyone stretches. Athletes do it before training and people in pain do it because most of the time it makes them feel somewhat better. However, the evidence on stretching shows it doesn't do half of what we think it does! This is pretty worrying considering how mainstream it has become over the last few decades. We had thought for many years that the plastic deformation theory was king, wherein we thought muscles changed length to account for increased muscle extensibility. However, as science challenges theories and conducts new research, things regularly get debunked and this is precisely what happened with stretching. Multiple studies showed that the new evidence just did not support this particular theory. Stretching does not change the length of tissue and in the absence of disease, there are only three ways you can change a muscle's length. You can contract the muscle, you can relax it, or you can go crazy on it with a scalpel, but I wouldn't recommend the last one! In fact, there are several muscles in your body that are biomechanically impossible to stretch fully as your own body parts get in the way! When you stretch your hamstrings, you will eventually hit a point where you can't go any further due to discomfort. If you start to go a little deeper, you may perhaps even get pain. However, if you relax for a few seconds, breathe a little, take a big breath in followed by a big breath out and slowly go deeper into the stretch, your brain can effectively turn down the discomfort and allow you further into the stretch or allow more of what is commonly referred to as range of motion (ROM). Ultimately though, we are not making the tissue longer, we are only modulating our nervous system to allow us to get further into the stretch. If you are a gold medallist gymnast who stretches every day, then the repetitive nervous system modulation is going to ensure that as soon as you go into that daily stretch, you are going to get close to that end range straight off the bat. However, if you have recently been told the nocebo of "you have a slipped disc" then you may find that you don't stretch very far at all due to inhibitory protective measures. This model of the stretching effect is referred to as the sensory theory and it is currently the only explanation, given the available evidence and what we know about stretching that explains it. There have been many myths about stretching that have been debunked by science. We now know that it doesn't warm you up before exercise, it doesn't prevent injuries and it doesn't stop soreness from exercise. However, it's not all doom and gloom as we do know that stretching is good for the heart. It stimulates enhanced vagal modulation (the effects of vagal nerve activity on the rate of the heart's contractions), something that becomes very important for the elderly or those with hypermobility.

Stretching also feels good and anything that feels good will release pain killing endorphins, something that we can definitely use to our advantage. Stretching is also very good at creating body awareness, it doesn't take any fancy equipment and it doesn't need prior experience to get started. Stretching is an excellent choice for our first foundation movement as it allows us to get used to the discomfort of the tissue and slowly adapt past that discomfort. Allowing yourself to feel the discomfort on purpose, along with seeing that it isn't doing any damage will massively help to reinforce everything you have learned thus far. Remember, it's not what we do (input), its how's its processed that matters. If we change how it's processed, then we change the output! When the time comes to get started, I would recommend three stretches in total; my kneeling hip flexor complex stretch and two stretches that you personally feel like you could do with if you feel "tight" or ones that you simply enjoy the feeling of.

Kneeling Hip Flexor Complex Stretch

One of two things are going to happen with this stretch. You will either get into it and the nociceptors at your knees will send the message that most of your body weight is being put through your knee and your brain with be just fine with that. However, more than likely, once that message gets to your brain it's going to evaluate everything and decide pain is probably an effective way to get you to stop kneeling! If this is you when you get into a kneeling position, then I'm going to take a guess that you have negative associations with knees. You may have been told you have osteoarthritis in your knees or hips, perhaps you have been conditioned over the years to avoid kneeling as it would cause pain in the past and reinforce the notion to stay off them. You may even dread the struggle to get back up again afterwards. Regardless of any of that, you still possess an incredibly strong pair of knees! A study conducted in 2015 found that hip pain is massively discordant with radiographic hip osteoarthritis. In the study they found that roughly 80% of people with the signs of arthritis had no pain! What's crazy though is that around 85% of people in the study who did have hip pain had no sign of arthritis! I want you to keep this in mind as we do this stretch. I use this in my foundations with clients as most have some problem bearing weight through their knees. Remember, whatever we do we get better at, the more you do this stretch, the easier it becomes. So much so that eventually kneeling without pain becomes the new normal.

Now, you won't hear me say that alignment matters very often, but this is going to be one of the times when it is important. However, its nothing to do with posture, it's just that you need to be nice and aligned so that you will be able to feel the stretch and bear your full weight properly.

How to do it

Kneeling on the floor with one foot out in front for support and bearing weight on the other knee, make sure you are nice and tall. The knee you are kneeling on should be directly below your hips, your hips should be directly below your shoulder and your shoulder should be directly below your earlobe. The leg out in front should have the foot firmly on the floor and your knee should be directly over your ankle. For most people, being in the position will be a little unstable, so for the first few time try using a wall for some support. Next, I want you to gently squeeze your bum so that your pelvis starts to tuck underneath. As soon as your pelvis tucks under you will feel a pull up the front of your thigh and some people may also feel it as far up as their stomach. Once you have the sensation of pulling, gently let the knee of your supporting leg move forward over your toes to help increase the feeling and then simply hold the position.

All of our stretches should be held for around the two-minute mark. Just relax and let your brain turn down the discomfort. Now, as you are doing this stretch please remember to breathe! Whilst holding the stretch you may find that you automatically hold your breath for added stability. If this is the case, then just try to relax and breath. The quicker you can do that, the quicker your brain can modulate your nervous system and the quicker the discomfort dials down. If you can, try and do the progressed version of this stretch with a cushion or small ball under the foot of the leg that's kneeling to help pull you into a little more flexion. In about six years of using this stretch, I've only known four people who haven't been able to start on the progressed version! It is far more likely to be fear that stops people in this stretch than anything biomechanical, please give yourself some credit and attempt it if you can.

Movements

The second part of our everyday movements will be a little more difficult. Over time you will have essentially been programmed to associate most movements or exercises with pain. Because of this, we have a lot of work to do in changing the processing of your movement in general. I want you doing movements, but they need to be transferable to everyday life. If you want to get good at playing the guitar, you wouldn't practice on a piano! The same is true for movement. Bridges are a good exercise to build up your bum muscles (glutes) and to help to get you stronger in movements like hip extension. However, the only time you use both bum muscles together with the same force that you do when you do a bridge, is when you get out of a chair or get off the toilet. Unfortunately, this is not hugely transferable to everyday life when we are trying to get you sitting less and moving more. It's even less transferable when consider 60% of walking is done on one leg. Now, don't get me wrong, there are no inherently bad exercises. Humans come in all shapes and sizes and some movements feel better for certain people depending on different factors. I just want you to be moving smarter. I don't want you to be working harder than you need to, I want you working smarter!

In my studio, depending on my client's individual history, fear, beliefs, etc, I would assign them to one of the four foundation programmes I made some time ago. However, without seeing you in person this is going to be a little more difficult. Because we can't physically see each other and spend time talking, I have put together a more generic version of some of the foundation movements I prefer for people to do. I would suggest the following examples for your everyday movements. If you have trouble getting the hang of them, you can find instructional videos of how to do them on my website in the "No Pain, No Pain" private sections, accessible by using the password "NOPAIN88"

Lean Overs

The lean over exercise is one of my personal favourites. It allows you to get stronger at contracting one side of your hip to help hold the other side up, effectively keeping your leg off the floor. Its massively transferable, as every step you take uses this pattern of movement to ensure your swing leg clears the floor when you walk. The less effort this takes, the more confident you will feel and therefore the more mobility you will be granted. To do the lean overs you need to find something that will let you... wait for it...lean over! I would suggest something that's about pelvis height, or at least thereabouts. Popular choices are a sofa arm, a kitchen bench, a dining table and as one of my clients once did, you could use your 7-year-old child lying on their side.

Lean over whatever it is you are using, make sure your feet are directly below your hips. Keep your left leg straight (those who are hypermobile, keep a very slight bend) and lift your right hip up gently whilst keeping your right leg straight until your right foot is one or two inches of the floor. Take your right leg out to the side, hold for one second and bring it back in to touch your left leg (keep the right foot off the floor always) and repeat. Once you have done a few repetitions, instead of taking your leg out to the side, take it out diagonally (out and back) and squeeze the bum cheek of the lifted leg on the way up. Once you have done a few repetitions, take your leg straight back and hold for two seconds. Bring it back down and once you have done a few repetitions, then swap legs. Repetition wise, we want something that is going to be hard enough to get your muscles uncomfortable, but not too many that you are too sore the next day to do them again. I would recommend 20 reps out to the side, 20 reps diagonally and 20 reps backwards...just don't forget to do the other side! Whilst you are doing this exercise you will feel it in the leg that's not moving. Remember, this is happening because the muscle is contracted to hold the opposite hip up whilst your leg is moving and it's a sign that you're doing it correctly.

Hinge Pattern

One thing I've noticed over the years whilst working with people who are in chronic pain is that their ability to hinge at the hip whilst performing certain movements leaves something to be desired. People in pain seem to have a tough time hinging. This can stem from things like mechanical coupling, fear, lack of stability, lack of mobility or a dip in proprioception from hyper lax tissues (like what happens to people who have Ehlers-Danlos Syndrome). Personally, I feel strongly that this is something that needs to be addressed if those in pain are ever to be able to move freely, confidently and without pain. The hip hinge allows you to create hip flexion and extension by hinging at the hips. With the hip hinge your spine stays straight and you bend at the hips instead of rounding the lower back. I experienced an episode where my brain turned off my ability to hinge not so long ago. I had just moved gyms and on my first visit noticed they had a plate loaded hack squat machine, which is something I had not seen for a while and something I have previously really enjoyed! I had a really good workout that day, pushed a little more weight that I normally would and left the gym in search of sustenance. The next morning however, I woke up a little bit stiff in my legs, hips and back from the gym, but thought nothing of it and went to work as normal. After about three hours of being at work I bent over to pick up a piece of paper from the floor and found I could no longer hinge. I was doing some crazy back rounding routine whilst making weird grumbling noises. Perhaps it was being stiff in new places that switched it off, perhaps it was the new gym environment, maybe it was the bad news I received that morning or even the fact there wasn't a lower back support on the machine like there is with most hack squats. Nonetheless, whatever it was, it was enough to stop me hinging for some reason. The next day I was fine and it was like nothing had ever happened.

Hinging at the hip whilst say, bending down to pick something up from the floor, is a darn useful movement pattern that we learn very early on. Most of us learn a variety of movement patterns by about two years old, such as the squat, push, pull, lunge, twist, etc. Hinging at the hips keeps us in a much better position mechanically to pick things up, utilising larger and more powerful muscles to perform the movement and effectively halving the workload. When we can't hinge effectively, it makes life much more difficult. People can find it incredibly hard to complete simply tasks like getting up or down from the floor. This, in turn, can lead people to create some very interesting and strange techniques to move around and these can increase the risk of falling. Please remember though that the spine is incredibly strong and picking up something light from the floor with a rounded back is very unlikely to cause damage or indeed pain. However, not being able to hinge at the hips does create some problems. It is likely to lead to you becoming less stable whilst picking things up and as we talked about earlier, when we don't feel stable, the brain can cut how much mobility we are allowed. Not being to hinge and being forced, repeatedly, to round our backs to pick things up, can irritate already sensitive nerves and drive us to protect ourselves via pain. Not being able to hinge also means that we become more like levers and those lower back extensor muscles must work twice as hard. Ultimately though, being able to hinge at the hip will open a world of confident, varied and pain free movement to you. Being able to hinge will make movements that were very hard to do, far easier almost instantaneously and this will help to reinforce the belief that you are capable of great pain free movement.

How to hinge

Stand up nice and tall with your feet shoulder width apart. Place your hands on your thighs with your arms straight. Whilst keeping your spine straight and your knees directly above your ankles (don't let them move) allow your hands to slide down your thighs as you gently push your bum backwards and placing your weight forward a little and hinging at the hips. This is a complicated movement and when you do it you may feel you're in the right position, even when you're not. I would recommend watching the video on how to do this movement. When you hinge, try and make sure you are not rounding your spine and stop when the palms of your hands are on your knee caps. Please keep in mind that certain drugs can affect your proprioception and knowing exactly where your joints are in the space around you may be difficult, but practice makes perfect. Now, time for the hard part! In this position, I want you to gently squeeze your bum as you hinge back up (keep squeezing until you get to the top), sliding your hands back up your thighs until you are back to the starting position. Please note that you need to make sure that this movement starts in the pelvis and that's what brings up the chest, which then brings up the head. When you can't hinge, people tend to lift their ribs up first and then their pelvis follows. We don't want to be using the lower back tissues as the primary mover, we want the bum to be the primary mover. I would personally start off with 30 repetitions of the hip hinge. Again, it's incredibly hard to explain movements via writing, so if you check out my website you can find a detailed video break down of the movement, which is far easier to understand.

Legs Up the Wall

After the movement parts have been done, I want you to build a strong association of feeling good after movement. So, as soon as you finished the last hip hinge, I want you to lie on the floor with your legs up the wall. There's a few reasons why this position is helpful for us. It inverts us to the force of gravity and allows our hearts to do less work whilst letting lymphatic waste drain easier from our legs. It's also a great relaxing position as it relaxes those lower back tissues now that they don't need to work very hard in this position. Despite all these fantastic reasons to do this pose to finish our movements, it's still not why we are going to do them. This position allows a different force vector to compress your spine, giving the feeling or sensation of your spine being stretched apart. Something that I hear a lot of from people with chronic pain is that they feel like there spine is being compacted and they spend a lot of time stretching in a bit to get the sensation of it being gently pulled apart and relieving the tension. Lying in this position takes the longitudinal compressive force off the spine.

As far as inputs go, this is one that most people will get the same output from, that being a feeling of looseness, relaxation and surprisingly, lower back pain relief. Remember though, anything that feels good releases pain killing endorphins. After you have finished your movements, allow yourself five minutes in the legs up the wall pose. End your movements with something that feels good and help to build that association that our everyday movement sessions can make us feel great!

Mairi: I totally agree here – this last movement is definitely my favourite! I won't lie. I was glad when these movements were finished. I wobbled, both physically and emotionally, throughout the sequences. I cried tears of frustration at how limited my movements were. But I did them, every day for two weeks. It wasn't pretty and thank goodness nobody filmed it, but making these movements put me back on the road to wellness. You will feel that you have moved in ways you haven't done for a while. You will feel that your muscles have been working. But it's a different feeling from the blinding agony of a flare up. Do it carefully and follow Adam's instructions and most important of all, don't give up! Remember, there are people to support you along the way in our online group.

Descending Modulation (Pin and Press)

Adam: I mentioned a few times in the last few sections about relaxing during stretches and letting your brain help to turn down the pain. Well, I did mean this quite literally! Imagine you are walking across the road and you fall and sprain your ankle. Whilst you're cursing out loud in obvious pain, a car comes screaming around the corner at a rapid speed. You suddenly jump up, run on your sprained ankle without any pain and soon find yourself safe on the other side. This is a good example of descending modulation in effect. The immediate danger is enough to trigger a survival response and allow pain to be modulated by the situation rather than have it cause even more damage by the car hitting you. We know that a few things like emotions, manual therapy and noxious stimuli, can all cause a descending modulation effect. This happens when several pain killing neurotransmitters such as opioids and GABA help to inhibit our experience of pain. As I've said many times in this book, whatever you do, you get better at and the more you create a situation in which you use descending modulation, the better you will get at doing it automatically. Surprisingly, we do have some emerging research that suggests that offering pain and neuroscience education to people with the fibromyalgia label can also produce a descending modulation effect long term. So, way to go! By simply reading and learning how strong the body is and how pain works you have already put the descending modulation train into motion! So, how are we going to create a noxious stimulus that we can turn down? Well, my clients will tell you this is the part where a slight grin appears across my face as I exclaim "Pin and Press my friend, Pin and Press".

Mairi: Shudder.

Adam: Where I would want you to pin and press is very much down to you as an individual. I normally go for the furthest away point from where you hurt the most. However, a lot of the time people say they hurt everywhere, in which case it doesn't really matter where we pin! For our pin and press we are going for two areas, the incredibly strong Iliotibial Band (ITB) and probably the most protected muscle for those in chronic pain, the Quadratus Lumborum.

The ITB is one long piece of non-contractile tissue that is anchored along the length of the femur. You simply cannot stretch it, release it or indeed really apply any force to it manually that's going to make any real long-lasting difference to the tissue. In all probability, it's likely to be easier to stretch the tyres on your car with your hands than it is to stretch the ITB. However, even with this knowledge, we still have people by the millions all foam rolling, trying to release or indeed stretch their ITBs in the hope of pain relief or a good tissue stretch. Some do succeed in feeling looser, gaining a perceived looseness or indeed pain relief, but we know it's more about the sensory theory and how our brains feel about the tissue rather than its length being changed. The ITB is flushed with lots of nerves and pinning this area is going to send a whole lot of potentially dangerous inputs to your brain. It sounds a little crazy, but this is what we want! I want you pinning this tissue and for every breath out, I want you to relax further into the pin and press, don't fight it. If you can relax and give in to it, something interesting happens around the 50 seconds to one-minute mark. The blunt dull initial ache will turn into a warm sensation which will then turn to pressure and eventually it will barely even register. Remember, throughout the whole time pinning the ITB, it remains the same input, but you get to feel the outputs change.

The Quadratus Lumborum is slightly different though. You are going to be incredibly protective of this area, so it might take some time to get used to this one. However, when you do get used to it, it can prove to be a very quick and effortless way to force yourself to relax that lower back tissue and create a sensation of sorely missed looseness in the area (no pun intended).

How to Pin and Press

ITB: For P+P in this area I would recommend using a broom handle or, if you're feeling adventurous, a small massage ball, although they are hard to stabilise on. Lie on your side on the floor nice and straight and lift yourself up gently to allow yourself to position the broom handle underneath you at around thigh level. Make sure you do not let your hips move forward or backwards, you should be hip on top of hip. I would usually say around two and a half minutes for P+P. Just keep your eyes open, breathe, hold for two minutes or so and repeat on the other side.

QL: This is rather tricky to pin as although your back is strong, I don't want you pinning your ribs, spine or hip when you do this. I would definitely urge you to watch the video on how to do this P+P before attempting it. The small massage ball is going to be placed in the middle of the Quadratus Lumborum muscle that connects your last rib to your pelvis. We don't want to put the ball too lateral so that the ball isn't sitting on anything, yet it shouldn't be so far in that it's on your spine. It also needs not to be too high and end upon you're the ribs or too low that it's on your pelvis. The ball needs to be right in the middle of the QL tissue.

Lie on the floor in a bridge position and lift your bum up to allow yourself to position the ball. I would recommend asking somebody to help you with the next bit, or you could use a wall. Gently pull your knees in towards your chest and whilst holding them in place, try to relax. Next, take a big breath in and as you breathe out roll slightly to the side that the ball is on. You will feel this pin and press sensation radiate. Just relax, breathe, hold for two minutes and repeat on the other side. After you do one side stand up. Notice how different both sides feel even though the tissue isn't any different! You will "feel" looser after this P+P press and will find you counter rotate when you walk much easier.

Mairi: You'll notice that I didn't say earlier that the movements we had done then were the worst bit. If you've tried these pin and press movements, you'll know why. These were worse than the cold showers for me. They were extremely unpleasant! But it's a funny thing, now I do them and I don't even need to because of the tension release they offer. Hilarious, I hear you say. No, they aren't fun whilst you are doing them but the relief they bring and the long term benefits they offer make every horrible bit worthwhile.

Progress Check

The final component is one that I really want you to keep on top of. It will help to keep you motivated on the days when you find it difficult. I want you to record how you feel about the movements, how you found them, what you enjoyed about them and what you didn't. By keeping a diary of your journey, you will be able to look back on it in a few weeks to get an objective view of how well you are doing. The same goes for video. Use your phone or any recording devices to film you doing your exercises and watch at how effortless they become in a mere few weeks.

Mairi: Honestly, if you've got this far, you have my undying respect. Both Adam and I both know how hard it is to follow through with these movements and if that wasn't bad enough, we are expecting you to do them every day for two weeks! It takes a huge amount of discipline and determination to grit your teeth and keep going when you're in pain and we applaud you for making this supreme effort. Well done but keep going!

Learning to Walk Again

Museum Walking

Adam: "You have to walk before you run" I'm certain we have all at some point in our lives heard this very common phrase. It does after all, make a lot of sense! Well, let me give you another saying that will make a little more sense, in the coming chapter "You have to have stability, before your body will give you mobility". In a previous chapter, we have talked about how posture isn't the big bad wolf it's been made out to be and we know that it doesn't really matter so much about how you sit or stand, you just have to move regularly. However, at the risk of causing a big old nocebo, there is something that I personally believe (and it comes up a lot in research), that you're probably doing when you walk that isn't really helping your situation and if we could just change it slightly, it would make a stark difference.

The best place to start when it comes to walking is to look at its history. Human beings have a very long and very complicated relationship with walking.

The oldest evidence for walking on two legs comes from one of the earliest humans known, *Sahelanthropus*, which dates back to nearly seven million years ago! However, many anthropologists remain sceptical of this and side with the extensive evidence for bipedalism for the 4.4-million-year-old *Ardipithecus Ramidus*.

There's a lot of theories as to "why" we evolved to walk on two legs, a phenomenon which is also knows as bipedalism. Suggestions range from climate change forcing our ancestors down from the trees, to freeing up the use of their hands and in turn helping them to form primitive tools and the fact that bipedal walking also helps to conserve energy, as walking on two legs takes far less energy than walking on all fours. In 2007 researchers studying chimpanzees on treadmills determined that the chimps required 75 percent more energy while walking than two-legged humans. Monkeys on a treadmill, now I have seen everything!

When you walk, and you step forward, you automatically rotate your pelvis a few degrees. The angular momentum from your arms swinging helps to counter rotate your thorax and you end up in a counter rotated state (thorax one way, hips another), its barely even that noticeable. However, extensive research shows us that people who are in pain adopt a protective walk in which they don't counter rotate a great deal at all. Some studies even show that people will adopt this protective walking pattern when sneaky specialist researchers tell them they have a bulging disc, even when they don't. The mere thought alone can be enough to create a different output, even though physically nothing has changed. Various beliefs that we hold about our backs, how weak we believe they are, how much pain we are in, how we feel today or simply awkward social situations, can ultimately change how we move. Have you ever noticed how differently you walk when you must walk past a crowd of people all looking at you? I bet you aren't slouched! So, if the way we move can be changed by different Biopsychosocial factors and being in chronic pain can stop us from efficiently counter rotating when we walk, then what does it mean? It means you are walking around expending energy, firstly to keep pain firing to keep you safe and secondly, using extra energy to effectively drag yourself though the environment instead of propelling yourself. Think about the difference between going for a four-hour hike and walking around museum for four hours. Although you do not cover anywhere near the same distance as hiking, walking around a museum for four hours is far more exhausting. In hiking, you are taking advantage of ground reaction force, dynamic walking, the environment and your own biomechanics in the form of counter rotation amongst other things. These all help to create a pendulum type of movement when you walk allowing you to take advantage of momentum. However, when walking around a museum, we walk more slowly, some of that ground reaction force gets wasted, we don't counter rotate a great deal and its ultimately harder getting from A to Z. At the end of the day, walking is not an exercise, it's a movement pattern, one that we have evolved to use a great deal of. So, for those of you reading this, chances are you are walking the way you would if you had walked around a museum all day! To be totally honest with you, if I were to walk around a museum all day I wouldn't want to exercise, I wouldn't want to do anything, I'd want to rest!

When walking, you need to understand that your spine is supposed to rotate. The spine is a beautifully curved and segment structure that gets its strength from its curves (much like Beyoncé). Each segment is capable of a different degree of rotation as we need each of them for different things. It should come as no surprise, then, that your cervical spine can rotate up to an amazing 90 degrees. Next up is the thoracic spine with an admirable 40 degrees. It's important to note that if you do become somewhat immobile at the thoracic spine, it's not uncommon to end up compensating elsewhere for the lack of rotation. Finally, we have your lumbar spine which can rotate up to 12 degrees. So, your lower back hasn't got anywhere near the same rotational capacity as the rest of your spine, but rightly so as it doesn't need that much. Your lumbar spine is meant to support the weight of the upper body, meaning it is designed more for stability than for massive amounts of rotation. However, this doesn't mean it shouldn't rotate. Given that the lumbar spine supports the upper body, should you feel unstable, protective or injured, you may find that this is the area that locks down to add more support.

Now, I'm not about to start giving you lessons in deportment or make you walk around your house with a book on your head, but I do want you to implement a few changes into how you walk;

1. Relax in your walking - Walking is stability in motion, its efficient, effortless and done with poise. We don't want you walking around like you're carrying a bag of potatoes! You are literally engineered through millions of years of evolution to walk, so relax through it and let your body know there is nothing to fear from walking.

2. Hurry up and slow down- A little bit of an oxymoron there huh? Speed hides a need for something that is lacking. If you are not very good at spelling, you may find your hand writing isn't that great as you subconsciously try to hide your spelling mistakes with illegible hand writing. The things we aren't very good at we tend to speed up to hide our shortcomings. Most people who don't feel very stable when they walk swap their normal stride lengths for shorter quicker ones! Let's make sure this isn't you! When

you walk allow yourself to pick up the speed a little bit and stride out spending longer on each leg. You know, hurry up and slow down!

3. Free up your ribs. If you're walking around slumped like you are being dragged around a museum, then you are going to find it hard to rotate. It can't rotate if it's not straight! So, what I suggest you do is to gently lift your sternum (breastbone). Don't pull your shoulders back, just lift your chest up. This allows you to open up your ribs, stop that mechanical coupling where your ribs and pelvis lock down and this will help you to use momentum when you walk.

Remember, when you walk you automatically propel yourself through the environment. You absorb the shock of landing on one leg and use it to propel yourself into the next step. Change how you move, and you will find that walking becomes less tiring and far easier.

Mairi: If I had one thing I hoped to get by consulting Adam, it was the ability to walk. It sounds so dramatic when I tell people that he taught me to walk again but it meant so much to be able to move well. I'd been in a wheelchair and had some unpleasant experiences there. All the usual things: not being able to access places I wanted to go, having people talk about me to the person pushing the wheelchair, getting parked somewhere near the bins which is the area for that had been set aside for "the disabled". No hidden message there I hope! Being able to walk again means I can actively join in with so many lovely activities. It helped me start to feel alive again. I hope it does the same for you.

But What if I Flare Up?

Adam: Now, this is a very good question. However, to answer this question we need to ask another one first! What exactly is a flare up?

A flare up is where Subconscious You flips the red alert button, activates “full protection mode“, rendering you effectively house bound or stuck in bed. A flare up is a very painful, incredibly inconvenient and hugely distressing output that we can all experience. However, it’s an absolute no brainer for Subconscious You, who, you may remember, has only one job to do and that’s to keep you safe. To help do that job they can condition us, over time, to do only the things that they perceive as safe for us. This could be in the form of lowering things like tissue tolerance which makes us create pain from things like our T-shirt simply rubbing on us, creating belief reinforcing outputs to change our behaviour or any other Bio-neurological response that’s going to create pain. This happens to help to condition us to stay away from things that “Subconscious You” perceives to be a danger to us.

You could say this is another form of Bioplasticity, but that it’s just acting in a more a negative way. Negative plasticity if you will! But then again, looking at it from the subconscious point of view, it’s a positive change in plasticity as it keeps you out of danger. If you have been in pain for more than six months you will have experienced this conditioning. At some point perhaps, you felt you were having a better day than you have had in a while and you decide to get some long overdue chores in the house done.

However, once done, you flared up and "ultimate protection mode" was engaged. This lowers tissue tolerance, increases your level of pain and you get conditioned to avoid the housework in the future. Just to reinforce the fact that Subconscious You thinks you have done a dangerous thing by attempting those chores, it can even go so far as to keep the tissue tolerance down as a long-term situation. So, doing things like a quick ten minutes of dusting would not have made you get anywhere near your tissues tolerance point previously. However, through that negative bioplastic change, your tissue tolerance is now lower. This means that by the time you get to five minutes of dusting, you are already in pain and forced to stop to avoid the catastrophic feeling of entering "ultimate protection mode".

Whatever it is that caused you to flare up, your brain has decided that you may have been getting a little too close to your tolerance level and has therefore flipped the switch. Your brain believed that it was doing this in your best interests. You may have consumed alcohol and pushed yourself a little bit too much; you may have already been in some sort of emotional distress beforehand or any other of the myriad of possible scenarios that could cause a flare up. However, it's important that you understand that a flare up is not damage! It is just a way for your brain to take control, keep you where it believes you are safe and condition you through Belief Reinforcing Outputs to avoid certain activities or situations. A flare up causes you to activate "full protection mode", releasing stress hormones, turning your sensitivity level to high, stopping your activity and thus keeping you safe. But like most things in life, if you understand them, then you can control them. Have you ever made a cup of tea for someone and gone to pick it up only for your hand to recoil back from a reflex act that's designed to protect you from excessive heat? You probably did what most of us would do and overrode that response by picking it back up again and quickly passing it to the person you made it for. A flare up is there to condition you, but it is you who is ultimately in control. By just understanding what it is and no longer demonising it and giving it power, you will find that it loses its omnipotent force over you.

So, this is my advice to the question "What if I flare up"

Out of everybody I work with throughout the year, pretty much nobody has had big flare ups from building a solid foundation. No, that's the right number! The foundation phase is going to keep you well under your tolerance level and the better you get at the foundation phase, the higher that tolerance level is going to get. In fact, as you start to feel better and become more and more in control, that level is going to keep getting higher. If something is notorious at flaring you up, think about what aspects of it are causing the flare up. If it is scrubbing the toilet on your hands and knees that does it, then do that for two minutes a day. Literally put aside two minutes of your day dedicated to quickly spending a little time on the floor scrubbing the toilet. More than likely because of the very small amount of time down there you will be fine. A few days later, extend the time to three minutes. As well as proving to yourself that you've overcome the negative bioplasticity that was previously "keeping you safe" you'll have a lovely pristine toilet floor! Everything you do either reinforces a belief or it breaks one down. So, start looking at things differently, break movement apart, take your time and take control. Every time you get down and scrub the toilet and you are ok, it breaks down that old belief that it's going to cause a flare up. You almost have to very slowly prove to your subconscious self that this is something that's fine to do.

Mairi: It's been a year since I began moving towards wellness with Adam and I can say, hand on heart, I've had no flare ups at all during that time. I've done some things I never imagined I would be able to do again and I've begun building my fitness levels back up again. Not once have I ended up in that excruciating, debilitating and frustrating state of flare up. Yes, I've had days when I've woken up a little stiff and sore in the morning, but that's because I'm moving in ways that I haven't done for years. Adam, very politely, describes this as being "deconditioned" but it's something I'm working on and getting better at. I have had no flare ups in over twelve months, but previously had suffered from these horrible experiences for more than ten years. After I had begun to move again, I remember asking Adam if it would be okay for me to go for a longer walk and would my body manage it. Adam told me I was thinking about it all the wrong way. It's my body and if I want it to take me for a walk, then it will do so. He told me to do it, take it slowly, relax and enjoy the new freedom. I did, it was wonderful and, though exhausted when I got home, it was definitely the turning point for me. I've never looked back and now that walk (which was two miles by the way) is my daily circuit, which I aim to complete a few seconds faster each time. No flare ups. Just controlled movement. And joy at the ability to move again after all these years.

D-Day

Adam: Alright, you now know everything you need to in order to finally get started! In the following paragraph I am going to go through an example of how you should implement what we have already discussed into your new daily routine. Now, a lot of people are going to be off to work during the day, but there are also a lot of people still working with the fibro diagnosis. If you are still working, follow the plan below as much as you can.

Upon Waking Up

I've said it a million times before that we need routine and I'm not going to stop now. Before alarm clocks were invented our ancestor used the big yellow one in the sky. In fact, our biology relies on having the sun there so that it can tell us when to go to sleep and when to wake up. When the sun is low in the sky the way that light refracts through the atmosphere means we are exposed to more orange/red light. This promotes the increased release of melatonin to make us tired and prepare us for sleep. When the sun is higher in the sky, light refracts much bluer and thus has the opposite effect. With this in mind, I want you to pick a time to get up and get up at that time every day. Give your brain a routine and give yourself more hours in the day. This will mean less stress to get things done and less stress means a more relaxed you. Getting up earlier also gives you a chance to become physically tired, meaning when you do go to bed, since it's been such a long day, you go to sleep and stay asleep. Now, you won't be used to being up early and its pretty much uncharted waters which, by the way, is a good thing. With having neither good nor bad associations with the early morning, it's a good first step to take as your brain is rather impartial about this time of day. Set a time to get up that's earlier than you are used to and get up at that time for most days of the week. This is going to be very hard at the start, so put your alarm clock at the other end of the room. This will force you to get out of bed, physically walk over to the alarm clock to turn it off. Then, once you're up, you're up.

Shower

Once up and after you have finished cursing me, give yourself ten minutes or so to adjust and then get in the shower. It's a brand-new morning so let's up that energy level, release some pain killing feelgood chemicals and start your day. Remember, get in a warm shower, have a little stretch and wake up fully, then slowly start turning that temperature dial down. Once you hit cold, breathe, relax and get through the next two minutes. Once you're done, feel free to make funny noises whilst running around cold and looking for your underpants.

Evaluate and Jot Down

So, you found those pesky underpants at last, excellent job! Now, it's time to sit down and take out your recovery journal. Your journal is a place to write down how you feel along your journey, what inputs seem to be causing problems, how it's going for you and it provides us with something tangible that can give us feedback. However, there is a more important reason why I want you to keep a diary. Our brains really like certain things in life. Things such as glucose and oxygen are ranked incredibly high, but the thing we are most interested with is the brains love of trying to predict the future. Brains use three things to try and predict the future; sensory information, beliefs and past experiences. We are using your journal as a sort of subconscious brain helper. By identifying potential problem inputs and finding solutions to them in advance, we are more prepared to deal with them rather than just firing off Protection Outputs willy nilly. When you sit down after your shower, get your journal out, think about the day ahead and try and find potential inputs that might occur during this day. Is there something that may potentially cause an output that you don't want, such as pain? The brother or sister that you are not particularly fond of may be coming around to visit later and this could then create an output that you don't want, for example. Use your journal to identify these inputs and sit down and think about how they are being processed to cause such a negative output. What's going on for you here? More importantly, what can you do to change that? A common input for me years ago that would cause a Protection Output would be public speaking. The sheer thought of public speaking would cause my neck to feel tight, pressure behind my eyes to build and this would eventually lead to a tension headache and that's just thinking about it, imagine what I was like on the journey there! To overcome this, I used to sit down and think about what I had to do that day that might cause a Protection Output that I didn't want. So, when it came to speak I would write down what I thought would influence the processing of the input of standing in front of lots of people all waiting for me to speak. In my journal I would write down that I wasn't hugely confident, so that would probably change how it was processed. I was also massively afraid of failure at the time which would definitely affect how I processed this input. To combat this, I wrote down what I needed to do to change it and then I did it. I watched a few YouTube videos on how to speak in public, I practised my speaking at smaller venues and I made sure I knew my presentations like the back of my hand. This all helped to make me feel much more confident. Remember, whatever we do we get better at. If you ever come to see me speak these days, you would think what I've just written is a lie. I am so confident in speaking because I've done so much of it. I have a laugh with the audience and I thoroughly enjoy talking. Use your journal first thing in the morning to identify the inputs of the day that may contribute to negative outputs, dissect how those inputs are going to be processed, change how they are processed. Ultimately, this will get you a totally different output.

Breakfast

To be eaten four hours after waking up. Over the years I have noticed one piece of anecdotal evidence: diet doesn't really seem to affect this process at all. I've had people keep strict diets whilst doing my programmes, I've had people eat what they want and yet really it doesn't seem to make any difference whatsoever. Perhaps as people begin to feel better, they spend more time cooking more nutritious meals and overcome any potential vitamin deficiencies. Perhaps deficiency in things like vitamin B12 and D are more of an effect rather than a cause. There is plausible evidence that certain dietary components could lead to things like abnormal Glutamatergic Neurotransmission, making those with the fibro label more sensitive to restricted diets. However, personally, I don't really think that diet makes an enormous difference at all. As you progress on your journey and begin to have more energy, then you can look towards creating a more balanced diet lifestyle. But, this early on, I don't think that restricting yourself and adding extra stress into your life is going to make things any easier for you, quite the opposite in fact. The benefits of eating food you enjoy far outweigh the negatives of restricting yourself during your journey or switching to less enjoyable food. Don't worry about meaningless things like weight. In fact, by simply just beginning to move again you will probably start to lose weight without trying. Please just eat the foods you enjoy, include lots of vegetables, drink plenty of water throughout the day and don't eat breakfast as soon as you get up. You will have just got out of a cold shower and have lots of blood forced deep towards your centre. Let that blood do something before we go and force it to help digest your breakfast. Let your body fully wake up first.

Mairi: Yay! Fine by me!

Sensory Turn Downs, Daily Movements and P+P

Adam: Now, this is where you need a shot of that self-discipline that we talked about earlier! You need to get your movements done and get them out the way before life can interfere, or before you start procrastinating. Don't do your sensory turn downs or movements last thing at night; make sure you get them done before 7pm. Ideally, you would do them around noon, but this isn't going to be possible for some people.

So, the running order of this part should look like this:

1. Kneeling hip flexor stretch - 2 ½ minutes per leg
2. A stretch that you feel you need or enjoy - 2 ½ minute per side (If applicable)
3. A stretch that you feel you need or enjoy - 2 ½ minute per side (If applicable)
4. Lean overs - 20 repetitions to the side, 20 diagonals and 20 backwards - Repeat on other leg
5. Hinge Pattern - 30 repetitions
6. Legs up wall pose - 5 minutes of pure bliss!

This means you should get through all the above in about 30 minutes (including rest time between), so not a huge amount of time to find every day to get them done. If you sit and watch television for more than 30 minutes a day then you have more than enough time to get these done every day. However, twice a week, I also want you to add in the pin and press.

So, twice a week your day will look like this;

1. Kneeling hip flexor stretch - 2 ½ minutes per leg
2. A stretch that you feel you need or enjoy - 2 ½ minute per side (If applicable)
3. A stretch that you feel you need or enjoy - 2 ½ minute per side (If applicable)
4. Lean overs - 20 repetitions to the side, 20 diagonals and 20 backwards - repeat on other leg
5. Hinge Pattern - 30 repetitions
6. Legs up wall pose - 5 minutes of pure bliss!
7. Iliotibial Band pin and press 2 ½ minutes per side
8. Quadratus Lumborum pin and press 2 ½ minutes per side

Time to F.E.A.S.T.

I want you to set aside some time every day to do something different, something that the Biopsychosocial you can feast on! F.E.A.S.T. stands for fun, educational, adventurous, social and terrifying. I want you to pick one and just do it. Now, some of them will mean different things to different people. However, whatever they mean to you, I want you to just go with it. You could call a friend or meet up, go out for dinner with your partner, learn something new, do something thoughtful for someone or try your hand at something scary at the weekend or even perhaps five minutes on the trampoline with kids. At the end of the day I want you to pick something from our acronym F.E.A.S.T. and simply do it. Push your boundaries and see how strong you truly are, because Mairi and I already know, you just need to show yourself that you can.

Reflect and Jot Down

This next part should be done right at the end of the day, preferably in bed. It's now time to start winding down for sleep and this is an important part for you as again, we need to set up another routine. Go to bed without the TV on, leave your phone on the other side of the room and get your journal out. Use the next twenty minutes or so to reflect on the day. Did you identify all the inputs that might cause bad outputs? Did you manage to find a solution to them or change how they were processed? If not, then why not? If you did, what was it that changed the processing? Use this time to get everything out of you head and into your journal, once you're done its time to go to sleep and let your body heal.

It's Your Move

Mairi: ...and that's all there is to it! Now that you've read this far, you know everything you need to get rid of this diagnosis of fibromyalgia once and for all and how to build the foundation on which to grow. Like hundreds of people before me, I followed Adam's advice and the results have been nothing short of miraculous. But this isn't some hocus pocus faith healing thing, nor is it a placebo effect. It took discipline, determination and sheer hard work. But it's a permanent change for the better to all the aspects of my life; the biological, the psychological and the social. I'll never forget the first time I flipped that tractor tyre. The excitement and joy that I felt when I achieved that movement was life changing. It was such a simple thing and I managed it after only a couple of hours of consultation. I learned exactly the same as what is laid out in this book and I took the decision to move towards wellness. Without a doubt, this is the best decision I have ever made.

I'm a psychologist. I have a PhD in Trauma Psychology and I read medical research and articles on a daily basis. I had access to all of the information that Adam had, but he made the link between the impact and consequence of a fibromyalgia diagnosis and the decline in physical and emotional wellbeing that happens as a direct result of this. Adam wasn't prepared to put up with a lifetime of being in pain so he set his mind to finding a way out of this horrible prospect. He found a recipe that worked and over the years, he has perfected that recipe to take into account the needs and differences of people of all ages and with a multitude of various health problems. After I had my consultation with Adam and worked through the programme, people often asked what he did and how I managed to get better. Truthfully, I wasn't completely sure at first. I just did what he recommended and watched as the pain receded and my energy increased. It wasn't till we wrote this book together that I fully understood the science behind his discovery. Now I can (hopefully) explain it clearly and pass on the information to anyone who wants to know how to shake off this horrible diagnosis.

I won't deny that it was difficult to keep doing what Adam recommended! Especially at first, there would often be floods of tears. It was painful at times, especially during the pin and press sections. I couldn't believe that doing these movements would make me better when every fibre of my being was telling me they would create a massive flare up and I would probably never walk again. I was frustrated at my lack of ability to do even the simplest movements. It's true to say that I'm not a natural athlete and sporting ability was never my strong point. Balance and grace don't come naturally to me and I hated feeling so inept. And don't even mention the early mornings and cold showers! The very thought still brings on an involuntary shudder. But it worked. And one year on it's still working. At the time of writing I'm 52 years old and I feel like a teenager. My strength is improving every day and I'm getting a life again after many years of sitting in pain, watching the world go by.

I've tried to tell as many people as I can about how they can get over the diagnosis of fibromyalgia and lead an active, pain free life. Many have been interested and positive about the experience, but some people have been vitriolic in their response.

My fibro couldn't have been as bad as their fibro, I was making up my symptoms and there was never anything wrong with me in the first place. These are all accusations that I've heard. It's a strange thing that not everyone encourages people who want to improve their lot in life. As someone who has had struggled with being ill and struggled to get better, I applaud anyone who makes the decision to change their life for the better. We all have the ability to make choices, and this book aims to give readers the knowledge to make choices that will give them their lives back, often after years of illness. I wish everyone all the success in the world, and I look forward to meeting you in our online forum!

Adam: We know that we cannot think away pain, as to do so would be to act consciously. What we do know however, is that everything we do either keeps our "book of life" the same, or it begins to rewrite the chapters within it. Use movement as your catalyst for change and let it positively affect all slices of your Biopsychosocial Pie. When you finish your foundations phase, there are a great many more steps to take, as this is only the beginning. From increasing your tolerance to exercise, breaking down the old wrong beliefs that you use to process inputs that create the outputs of pain, to going back to work and embarking on the next stages of your recovery after you have laid your foundation. There is a long road ahead and the main purpose of this book was to show people that recovery is possible. This foundation phase will allow you to build a strong base from which to take your next steps. When that time comes, you will find Mairi and myself waiting for you in the private section of the site. If you have any questions or you need a helping hand, we are both only a message away. I wish you luck, self-discipline and courage on your journey ahead and I leave you with the motivational words of my old sergeant:

A comfort zone is a beautiful place, but nothing ever grows there.

Bibliography

Anderson, R.C., Reynolds, R.E., Schallert, D.L. & Goetz, E.T. (1977). Frameworks for comprehending discourse, *American Educational Research Journal*, 14(4), 356-381

Apkarian, A.V., Bushnell, M.C., Treede, R. & Zubieta, J. (2012), Human brain mechanisms of pain perception and regulation in health and disease, *European Journal of Pain*, 9(4), 463-484

Ashgari, A. & Nicholas, M.K. (2001), Pain self-efficacy beliefs and pain behaviour. A prospective study, *Pain* (94), 85-100

Bandura, A. (1989). Regulation of cognitive processes through perceived self- efficacy. Developmental Psychology. 25(5). 729-735

Body in Mind Research Group, Research into the role of the brain and mind in chronic pain. University of South Australia www.bodyinmind.org

Bortz, W.M. (1984), The disuse syndrome, *Western Journal of Medicine,* 141(5), 691-694

Crombez, G., Eccleston, C., Van Damme, S., Vlaeyen, J. & Karoly, P. (2012). Fear-avoidance model of chronic pain: the next generation. *The Clinical Journal of Pain,* 28(6), 475-483

Daley, A.J., Grimmett, C., Roberts, L., Wilson, S., Fatek, M., Roalfe, A. & Singh, S. (2008). The effects of exercise upon symptoms and quality of life in patients diagnosed with irritable bowel syndrome: a randomized controlled trial, *International Journal of Sports Medicine*, 29, 778-782

Eccleston, C. & Crombez, G (1999). Pain demands attention: a cognitive-affective model of the interruptive function of pain, *Psychological Bulletin*, 125(3), 356-366

Falck, R.S., Davis, J.C. & Liu-Ambrose, T. (2017), What is the association between sedentary behaviour and cognitive function? A systematic review, *British Journal of Sports Medicine*, 51, 800-811

Eysenbach, G., Powell, J., Englesakis, M., Rizo, C. & Stern, A. (2004) Health related communities and electronic support groups: systematic review of the effects of online peer to peer interactions, BMJ, 328:1166

Farinatti, P.T., Brandao, C., Soares, P.P. & Duarte, A.F. (2011). Acute effects of stretching exercise on the heart rate variability in subjects with low flexibility levels, *Journal of Strength and Conditioning Research*, 25(6), 1579-1585

Fayaz, A., Croft, P., Langford, R.M., Donaldson, L.J. & Jones, G.T. (2016). Prevalence of chronic pain in the UK: a systematic review and meta-analysis of population studies. *BMJ Open* 2016;6:e010364

Festinger, L. (1956) A Theory of Cognitive Dissonance. Stanford University Press, California

Gatchel, R.J., Peng, Y.B., Peters, M.L., Fuchs, P.N. & Turk, D.C. (2007). The biopsychosocial approach to chronic pain: specific advances and future directions, *Psychological Bulletin*, 133(4), 581-624

Gibson, J.N., Grant, I.C., Waddell, G. (1999). The Cochrane review of surgery for lumbar disc prolapse and degenerative lumbar spondylosis, *Spine,* (24): 1820-1832

Giesecke, T., Graceley, R.H., Grant, M.A.B., Nachemson, A., Petzke, F., Williams, D.A. & Clauw, D.J. (2004). Evidence of augmented central pain processing in idiopathic chronic low back pain, *Arthritis & Rheumatology*, 50(2), 613-623

Gillanders,D.T., Ferreira, N.B., Bose, S. & Esrich, T. (2012). The relationship between acceptance, catastrophizing, and illness representations in chronic pain. European Journal of Pain. 17(6), 893-202

Graceley, R.H., Geisser, M.E., Giesecke, T., Grant, M.A.B., Petze, F., Williams, D.A. & Clauw, D.J. (2004). Pain catastrophizing and neural responses to pain among persons with fibromyalgia, *Brain,* 127(4), 835-843

Guillot, X., Tordi, N. Mourot, L., Demougeot, C., Dugue, B., Prati, C. & Wendling, D. (2014). Cryotherapy in inflammatory diseases: a systematic review. *Expert Review of Clinical Rheumatology*, 10:2, 281-294

Hill, J.A. & Olson, E.N. (2008). Cardiac plasticity, *New England Journal of Medicine*, 358(13), 1370, 1380

Institute for Chronic Pain: What is the neuromatrix of pain? https://www.instituteforchronicpain.org/understanding-chronic-pain/what-is-chronic-pain/neuromatrix-of-pain

Kay, A.D. & Blazevich, A.J. (2012). Effect of acute stretch on maximal muscle performance: a systematic review. *Medicine & Science in Sports & Exercise,* 44(1), 154-164

Knobloch-Westerwick, S. & Meng, J. (2009), Looking the other way: selective exposure to attitude-consistent and counterattitudinal political information, *Communication Research*, 36(3), 426-448

Laimi, K, Mäkilä A, Barlund, E., Katajapuu N., Oksanen, A., Seikkula, V., Karppinen, J. & Saltychev, M. (2018). Effectiveness of myofascial release in treatment of chronic muscoskeletal pain: a systematic review, Clinical Rehabilitation, 32(4), 440-450

Lederman, E. (2010). The myth of core stability, *Journal of Bodywork and Movement Therapies*, 14(1), 84-98

Macfarlane, G.J., Kronisch, C., Dean, L.E., Atzeni, F., Hauser, W., Fluss, E., Choy, E., Kosek, E., Amris, K., Branco, J., Dincer, F., Leino-Arjas, P., Longley, K., McCarthy, G.M., Makri, S., Perrot, S., Sarzi-Puttini, P., Taylor, A. & Jones, G.T. (2017). EULAR revised recommendations for the management of fibromyalgia. *Annals of the Rheumatic Diseases*, 76, 318-328

Maguire, E.A., Wollett, K., Gadian, D.G., Johnsrude, I.S., Good, C.D., Ashburner, J., Frackowiak, R.S.J. & Frith, C.D. (2000), Navigation-related structural change in the hippocampi of taxi drivers, *Proceedings of the National Academy of Sciences of the United States of America,* 97(8), 4398-4403

Malik, S.H. & Coulson, N.S. (2010). Coping with infertility online: an examination of online self-help mechanisms in an online fertility support group. Patient Education & Counseling, 81(2), 315-318

Mosely, L. (2014) It is not just the brain that changes itself – time to embrace bioplasticity?

www.bodyinmind.org/time-to-embrace-bioplasticity/

Namerow, L.B., Kutner, E.C., Wakefield, E.C., Rzepski, B.R. & Sahl, R.A. (2016). Pain amplifications syndrome: a biopsychosocial approach. *Seminars in Pediatric Neurology*, (23), 223-240

National Health Service Choices (2017). Injuries due to falls in people aged 65 and over

https://www.nhs.uk/Scorecard/Pages/IndicatorFacts.aspx?MetricId=8135

National Institute for Health and Care Excellence https://www.nice.org.uk/

Okifuji, A. & Turk, D.C. (2017). Engagement of patients in the self-management of pain, in O'Donohue, W., James, L. & Snipes, C. (eds) Practical Strategies and Tools to Promote Treatment Engagement, Springer, USA

Oliveira, E.P. & Burini, R.C. (2009) The impact of physical exercise on the gastrointestinal tract, *Current Opinion in Clinical Nutrition & Metabolic Care*, 12(5), 533-538

Owen, A.M., Hampshire, A., Grahn, J.A., Stenton, R., Dajani, S., Burns, A.S., Howard, R.J. & Ballard, C.G. (2010), *Nature,* 465, 775-778

Panza, F., D'Introno, A., Colacicco, A., Capurso, C., Pichichero, G., Capurso, S.A., Capurso, A. & Solfrizzi, V. (2006). Lipid metabolism in cognitive decline and dementia, *Brain Research Reviews*, 51(2), 275-292

Quintner, J.L., Bove, G.M. & Cohen, M.L. (2015). A critical evaluation of the trigger point phenomenon, *Rheumatology*, 54(3), 392-399

Roussel, N.A., Nijs, J., Meeus, M., Mylius, V., Fayt, C. & Oostendorp, R. (2013). Central sensitization and altered central pain processing in chronic low back pain. Fact or myth? *Clinical Journal of Pain*, 29(7), 625-638

Schuh-Hofer, S., Wodarski, R., Pfau, D.B., Caspani, O., Magerl, W., Kennedy, J.D. & Treede, R.D. (2013). One night of total sleep deprivation promotes a state of generalized hyperalgesia: A surrogate pain model to study the relationship of insomnia and pain, *Pain,* 154(9), 1613-1621

Schrier, I. (1999). Stretching before exercise does not reduce the risk of local muscle injury: a critical review of the clinical and basic science literature, *Clinical Journal of Sports Medicine*, 9(4), 221-227

Seminowicz, D.A. & Davis, D.A. (2006). Cortical responses to pain in healthy individuals depending on pain catastrophizing, *Pain*, 120, 297-306

Thacker MA, & Moseley GL (2012). First-person neuroscience and the understanding of pain. *The Medical Journal of Australia, 196* (6), 410-1 PMID: 22471546

Tiidus, P.M. (1997). Manual massage and recovery of muscle function following exercise: a literature review, *Journal of Orthopaedic & Sports Physical Therapy,* 25(2), 107-112

Tversky, A., Kahnerman, D. (1974), Judgement under uncertainty: heuristics and biases, Office of Naval Research

Ulrich, P. (2017). Pain, in Budd, M.A., Hough, S., Wegener, S.T. & Stiers, W. (Eds) Practical Psychology in Medical Rehabilitation, Springer International Publishing

Van Euden-Kraan, C.F., Drossaert, C.H.C., Shaw, E.T.B.R., Seydel, E.R. & van de Laar, M.A.F.J. (2008). Empowering processes and outcomes of participation in online support groups for patients with breast cancer, arthritis or fibromyalgia. Qualitative Health Research, 18(3), 405-417

van Wilgen, C.P., van Ittersum, M.W., Kaptein, A.A. & van Wijhe, M. (2008). Illness perceptions in patients with fibromyalgia and their relationship to quality of life and catastrophizing. Arthritis & Rheumatology, 58(11), 3618-3626

Vlaeyen, J.W.S. & Morley, S. (2005). Cognitive-behavioral treatments for chronic pain. What works for whom? *Clinical Journal of Pain*, 21(1), 1-8

Vogel, H. (2009). Nervous System, Cambridge university Press, Cambridge.

Weppler, C.H. & Magnusson, S.P. (2010). Increasing muscle extensibility: a matter of increasing length or modifying sensation? Physical Therapy, 90(3), 438-449

Wiech, K., Ploner, M. & Tracey, I. (2008). Neurocognitive aspects of pain perception, *Trends in Cognitive Science*, 12(8), 306-313

Index

Aristotle 39

attention..48, 56, 64, 73, 117

autonomic nervous system.......................................58, 59

balance...136, 172

barriers 106, 118, 120, 141

belief 59

belief dismantling output...59

belief reinforcing output 52

beliefs....30, 37, 41, 43, 44, 45, 53, 54, 56, 60, 61, 62, 63, 64, 67, 68

bioplasticity...........................84, 87, 88, 91, 162, 166, 196, 198

biopsychosocial 40, 41, 102, 147, 153, 162, 192, 207, 211

book of life 43, 45, 46, 50, 52, 69, 85, 86

brain fog 79, 123

brain training...88, 89

central nervous system...44, 58

chronic pain...9, 21, 27, 31, 35, 47, 49, 51, 60, 61, 63, 70, 82, 91

clinical guidelines...32

cognitive dissonance 54, 60, 62

cold showers.......................................166, 169, 170, 189, 210

commitment 158

confirmation bias 53

conflict 54, 60

congenital analgesia....................39

coping....................72

culture....................41

damage 39, 50, 52, 56, 63

danger 37, 44, 45, 48, 50, 51, 53, 57

deconditioning 56, 79

dementia....................27, 79

Descartes 39

descending modulation....................185

diagnosis 32

diet....................82, 203

digestive problems....................81

dissonance.................... See cognitive dissonance

Ehlers-Danlos Syndrome....................125, 181

exercise 33, 54, 80, 81, 82

experience....................31, 35, 37, 44, 45

fear 21, 55, 56, 69, 73, 74

feel-good chemicals....................37, 45, 56

flare up....25, 56, 94, 96, 120, 125, 153, 157, 159, 164, 167, 169, 185, 196, 197, 198, 199, 210 goals 111, 140

graded exercise 32

heuristics 45

hippocampus 88

homeostatis 59

hormones 44, 57, 82

immune system 84

injury 21

inputs 37

inputs and outputs 35

Irritable Bowel Syndrome 81

Itching 82

journal 64, 80, 173, 190, 202, 207

limbic system 48, 49

massage 37, 145, 146

memory 31, 43, 79, 88, 89

mood 37, 55, 56

mood output 55

movement....22, 33, 57, 63, 79, 80, 81, 82, 91, 118, 119, 120, 133, 135, 136, 138, 143, 144, 146, 147, 153, 155, 157, 158, 159, 161, 162, 164, 170, 172, 175, 178, 179, 182, 183, 184, 185, 193, 198, 199, 209, 211

muscles 44, 56, 57, 79, 124, 131, 133, 136

Myalgic Encephalomyelitis 123

nerves...39, 58, 85, 86, 87

neuroplasticity...88

opinions 53, 60

outputs....36, 37, 39, 41, 43, 44, 45, 46, 48, 49, 50, 52, 55, 57, 59, 62, 63, 65, 66, 68, 86, 87, 91

pacing 77

pain centre 47

pain receptors 39, 47

pain threshold 47

parasympathetic nervous system 58

plastic deformation theory 173

posture 21, 24, 135, 136

prefrontal cortex 48, 49

procrastination 115

prognosis 32

protection output.......................44, 46, 50, 51, 52, 57, 59, 63

Protection Output 63

Psychophysiological Reconditioning Education Training 35

range of motion 131, 174

Schema Theory 45

sea squirt 160

self-esteem....33, 117, 141, 148
sensory turn down....205
side effects....82
sleep....80, 81
slipped disc....143, 174
somatic nervous system....58
somatosensory....48, 49
spinal flexion....143
spinal stability....136
spinal subluxation....144
Spoon Theory....77
stress....44, 57, 70
stretching....137, 173, 174, 175, 184
subjective world view....29
subsidiary output....57, 59
support groups....62, 101, 102, 103, 104, 105, 106
threat....41, 44, 45, 50, 52, 58, 59, 63
tissue damage....40
tissue tolerance....196, 197
trauma....9, 39, 51
trigger points....145, 146

ultimate protection mode 196, 197

walking 33, 71, 77, 127, 140

weak core 126, 136, 144

Printed in Great Britain
by Amazon

59052494R00129